Forever Hold Your Banner High!

Forever Hold Your Banner High!

The Story of the Mickey Mouse Club and What Happened to the Mouseketeers

by Jerry Bowles

DOUBLEDAY & COMPANY, INC.
GARDEN CITY, NEW YORK
1976

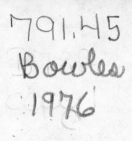
Grateful acknowledgment is made to Charing Cross
Music, Inc., for permission to quote lines from "An
American Tune" by Paul Simon. Copyright © 1973
by Paul Simon.

Portions of this book appeared in *Esquire*, copyright
© 1976 by Esquire, Inc., and in *Acquire*, copyright
© 1975 by Acquire Publishing Company, Inc.

ISBN: 0-385-11622-5
Library of Congress Catalog Card Number: 75-40712
Copyright © 1976 by Jerry Bowles
ALL RIGHTS RESERVED
PRINTED IN THE UNITED STATES OF AMERICA
FIRST EDITION

Everyone who regularly watches the "Mickey Mouse Club" television show is automatically a member of the Mickey Mouse Club and a Mouseketeer First-Class in good standing.

WALT DISNEY

Know Thyself, a wise old Greek once said. Know Thyself. Now what does this mean, boys and girls? It means be what you are. Don't try to be Sally or Johnny or Fred next door; be yourself. God doesn't want a tree to be a waterfall, or a flower to be a stone. God gives to each of us a special talent. God wants some of us to become scientists, some of us to become artists, some of us to become firemen and doctors and trapeze artists. And He gives each of us the special talents to become these things, provided we work to develop them. We must work, boys and girls. So: Know Thyself. Learn to understand your talents and then work to develop them. That's the way to be happy.

JIMMIE DODD, *a Doddism, 1955*

I don't know a soul that's not been battered
I don't have a friend who feels at ease.

I don't have a dream that's not been shattered
Or driven to its knees.

PAUL SIMON, *An American Tune*

ROLL CALL

RED TEAM

Sharon Baird
Bobby Burgess
Lonnie Burr
Tommy Cole
Annette Funicello
Darlene Gillespie
Cheryl Holdridge (*Second Year*)
Cubby O'Brien
Karen Pendleton
Doreen Tracey

THE GROWN-UPS

Jimmie Dodd
Roy Williams
Bob Amsberry

BLUE TEAM

Don Agrati
Sherry Allen
Nancy Abbate
Billie Beanblossom
Johnny Crawford
Dennis Day
Eileen Diamond
Dickie Dodd
Mary Espinosa
Bonnie Lynn Fields
Judy Harriet
Linda Hughes
Dallas Johann
Lee Johann
Bonnie Kern
Charles Laney
Larry Larsen
Paul Peterson
Lynn Ready
Mary Lynn Sartori
Bronxon Scott
Michael Smith
Jay Jay Solari
Ronald Steiner
Margene Storey
Mark Sutherland
Don Underhill

ACKNOWLEDGMENTS

The persons most responsible for the publication of this book are Betsy Nolan, a friend who believed in the viability of the project and made it happen, and Lawrence P. Ashmead, an extraordinary editor who knows a halfway decent book when he sees one. The person most helpful in writing the book is Mouseketeer Lonnie Burr who wishes I'd stop calling him that. The person most responsible for making me happy is my wife, Suzanne.

And, finally, the person who has been most helpful to my writing career is Don Erikson of *Esquire* who edits the best magazine in America and has been known, in weaker moments, to publish something I've written in it.

FOREWORD

There are a few things you ought to know before you plunge into this eccentric little volume. Since this book was written, the "Mickey Mouse Club" has gone into syndication again. A couple of more or less "official" books (meaning they were compiled with the aid and blessing of Walt Disney Productions) have appeared. Rumor has it that Disney is preparing a new "Mouse Club" for sometime next year.

This book was written without official sanction and with occasional objections. The research was done at a time when almost nobody was interested in the subject. If I may seem immodest, I suspect that my snooping around may have inspired a few other people to get interested.

This is not a "they lived happily ever after" kind of book and the length of time it has taken to appear in print is a kind of testament that it is not an easy book to love. It is as honest as I can make it.

Because it is about young, active people the facts change constantly. Among the changes that I know about: Annette has had another baby, a boy named Jason; Cheryl has remarried; Lonnie has moved back to the Coast; Tommy has quit KNBC to become a free-lance makeup artist. However, I don't think the basic facts—the substance of the characters' lives—have changed that much.

CONTENTS

1

The Middle-Class Dream

There are few cities in the world with as well defined a sense of economic geography as Los Angeles. The reason this is so is because it is a city in a desert near mountains and an ocean. Where there is a city in a desert near mountains and ocean, the mountains and ocean are prized most. This is true everywhere, but in Los Angeles, where the measure of a man is the machine he rides in, it is particularly true.

This unique status arrangement begins at the top with Bel Air, which has the best of both mountains and sea, descends into the elegant hidden villas of Beverly and Holmby Hills, the manicured lawns of Hancock Park, and climbs back up again into the Hollywood hills near the Beverly Hills border. In Westwood, this natural economic classification settles into solid middle-class comfort, goes tacky in Hollywood itself, and becomes miserable downtown on the desert floor.

All else is the Valley. The San Fernando Valley, L.A.'s bedroom on the other side of the Santa Monica mountains, a sprawling crazy quilt of subdivision homes, backyard wading pools, off ramps, drive-in banks, restaurants, movies and churches, used-car lots and E-Z credit hawkers catering to every conceivable want. Spiritually, it is a vacuum, devoid of a sense of neighborhood or general philosophic direction. The glue that holds it all together is ambition, the hope for a better life, a house higher up the hill. Up there among the stars.

Over eight million people live in the Los Angeles basin which covers all of Los Angeles and about half of Orange County. It is second only to New York in population, second to none in sprawl.

The Valley is the personification of the dream of middle-classhood, although it does have its small contradictions. Comedian Bob Hope, one of California's wealthiest men, lives in the Valley, in Toluca Lake. Walt Disney lived there and chose to move his studio to Burbank in the early fifties. Universal Pictures is in the Valley as are most of the other movie companies and television dream factories.

Perhaps, this is not really a contradiction at all. The dream of becoming a film or television star is a middle- or working-class ambition, after all. And despite his affection for polo, Walt Disney remained the dour son of a Missouri farmer with no patience for either intellectualism or status arrangement. Disney simply chose to live among the people who most revered his vision of the American dream. In a sense, he was simply living over the store. The Valley was his spiritual home.

How inviting this Valley must have seemed to those thousands of settlers who came west in those giddy, heroic, brave new world days following World War II. Tract homes. No down. G.I. bill.

They settled in places with exotic names: Van Nuys, Studio City, Sherman Oaks, Burbank. The new pilgrims brought with them the security of a world finally at peace and the certainty of prosperity to come. Who cared if some intellectual had labeled it "Iowa with palm trees," this was the good life. God smiled on America in those days. For these survivors of the Great Depression and the Big War, life would be different under the golden sun. Their kids would have the advantages they had missed. They had a shot at the silver screen. Certainly, they would never know hunger or fear. They would have dance lessons.

The new fantasy was television which, although still in its infancy in the early 1950s, was already beginning to reshape the entertainment business. Many of the major studios, feeling the pinch of dwindling box office receipts, were reluctantly moving toward television. Twentieth Century Fox, for example, began putting together a series based on the old Roddy Mac-Dowell classic *My Friend Flicka*, with a young Canadian named Johnny Washbrook in the lead role.

"All the major studios were just feeling their way," says Washbrook, now an actor in New York. "Twentieth tried to put the same amount of production quality into the series as they had put in their movies. As a result, 'Flicka' was an extremely expensive show to produce. We only made forty-nine episodes all together but it played for thirteen years on all three networks at one time or another."

The state of television programming for children was rather poor in 1954, although perhaps no worse than the Saturday morning fare of today. There was another horse series called "Fury" which starred Bobby Diamond, now a lawyer in Los Angeles. There was "Pinky Lee" ("Yoo hoo, it's me. My name is Pinky Lee.") There were a bunch of "Romper Rooms" across the nation and they all seemed to presume that kids were idiots. There was "Captain Corbett" and "Sky King" with Kirby Grant. And, of course, there was the venerable "Howdy Doody" with Buffalo Bob which had been in regular production since 1947.

It was simplistic stuff, to be sure. But then, the 1950s was a rather simple decade, at least on the surface. It is hard now, in modest retrospect, to picture a world as innocent as those golden days when the good general ran the nation from the ninth tee at Augusta, popping into view only occasionally to dazzle the nation with a malapropism or two. "It was a rather comforting thing to have this labor leader saying this, when we had so many wise-cracking so-called intellectuals going around and showing how wrong was everybody who don't happen to agree with them," he said one bright day in Los Angeles and not a soul standing there in the mothering California sun bothered to disagree.

It was the dawning of the age of the consumer. Through the miracle of television advertising and our national mania for creating products, it was suddenly possible to want things that didn't even exist a few years earlier. The path to the Good Life seemed so clear: a college education, a steady nine-to-five job with a good retirement plan, a house in the suburbs, kids, shaggy dogs, campers, a little wife in a big kitchen.

It was, we sometimes think, the best of times—a generation of peace, prosperity, and promise. And although we now know it as a false peace and a false promise . . . well, who can remember his white bucks or ducktail without going a little misty? In retrospect, we now know that the fun we had with the police in Fort Lauderdale was a sign of something deeper, darker, and more sinister in our restless national consciousness. Those people who got on the buses in Birmingham suddenly didn't just want to sit up front; they wanted the whole bus. In our feverish attempts to catch the Russians in science after Sputnik, we created a generation of slide-rule zombies.

Black liberation, women's liberation, gay liberation; Kennedy, Malcolm X, Kennedy, Rockwell, King, Attica, Da Nang, Hue, Columbia, Kent State, Jackson State, and so on. The banner dipped low in the sixties.

The triumphs of the 1950s stand revealed before us now like exhibits at an inquest: 1950—Diner's Club, the first credit card is born; 100 TV stations are operating in thirty-eight states; 1952—The word babysitter appears in the dictionary; 1953—Air travel has become one quarter of the railroad-bus figure; 1954—The TV dinner makes its appearance; the first twenty computers are delivered to American industry; the hydrogen bomb is perfected; 1955—Television advertising hits $1 billion; Charlie Parker dies; Fort Lauderdale erupts; 1956—Elvis goes into the Army; *Playboy* is founded; James Dean dies in an automobile accident; 1957—The Russians launch Sputnik; 1958—NASA is born; sale of tranquilizers hits the $2 million mark.

But, at the time, the national mood was one of optimism. The nation was firmly on the road to the great society. The working-men, the people of the Valley, would finally have the life they deserved. It seems only natural, in retrospect, that when Walt Disney reluctantly agreed to produce the "Mickey Mouse Club" for ABC, he would look no farther than his own backyard for the talent. The San Fernando Valley represented the triumph of the working class. It was a microcosm of blue collar America and out of this microcosm a few would be chosen to be stars.

In the early months of 1955, the word went out. Walt Disney is looking for kids to appear on a new TV series. He wants just normal, average, everyday kids. The auditions are open. Anybody can come.

* * *

Let us pause for a moment to meet the writer. I watched the "Mickey Mouse Club" on WDBJ, a Roanoke, Virginia, station which was about two hundred miles southeast across the Appalachians from where I lived in southern West Virginia. It was the closest station. Because of the distance, the picture signal was weak and snowy and I spent most of my teen-age Saturdays moving the outside antenna around in an endlessly futile attempt to improve the reception.

I was twelve years old in 1955—the same age as Annette and Lonnie. Starting to get pimples. They were called "zits" in West Virginia. I'm not sure what they were called where you were.

We got our first television set, an incredibly durable second-hand Zenith, the summer before the Mouseketeers. It was fascinating, this little electronic box that sat in a corner and brought in the outside world. I would often sit and watch the test pattern.

Before we had a set, my family used to go every Friday night to my Uncle Edgar's house to watch his. It was a big night on the little screen.

There was John Cameron Swayze with the news; "Coke Time with Eddie Fisher"; "Shenna—Queen of the Jungle"; "I Led Three Lives," and "Life of Riley." ("What a revoltin' development this is.") Most of all, though, there was the Friday Night Fights.

It is hard to imagine a world as innocent as mine in 1955. There wasn't even a lock on the front door of our house.

I fell in love with Annette Funicello at first sight. She made my chest hurt. I didn't pay much attention to her in the regular Mouseketeer sequences of the program but her role in "Spin & Marty" sent me into an exaltation of passion. I thought about her constantly.

I hated farming, still do. I wince when my friends in the city tell me about this marvelous little place they have just bought in the Berkshires. I prefer food that comes out of boxes.

Once I could name all the former American Presidents. I read, and believed, J. Edgar Hoover's book about how the commies were taking over and how he, Hoover, was going to stop them. I believed in God, in the moral superiority of America over every other country in the world. When I graduated from high school, I was awarded an American Legion Good Citizenship citation and a Danforth Foundation "I Dare You" award.

* * *

Walt Disney didn't want to do the "Mickey Mouse Club." He never wanted to do it and never liked the show very much after it was done. His major obsession during the early and middle months of 1955 was the opening of his fantasy amusement park, Disneyland, out in the orange groves of Anaheim. He had neither the time, nor the inclination, to devote to the launching of a daily children's television show. But, the American Broadcasting Company—encouraged by the commercial and viewer success of "Disneyland-TV," the Disney nighttime show launched in 1954 and the forerunner of today's "Wonderful World of Color"—wanted it and ABC was not only willing to foot the bill (to the tune of a $1 million revolving fund for the studio to turn out the show as quickly as possible), but they also agreed to lend Disney $1.5 million toward financing the completion of Disneyland. It was money Disney could scarcely pass up since a lot of his bankers were getting increasingly nervous about his grandiose Orange County dream.

Disney's basic attitude toward television, never a secret, was that it was hardly a worthwhile venture in itself but regular programming had enormous potential as a promotional vehicle for his theatrical releases and for the park. That's why he had agreed to do "Disneyland-TV." Now, ABC wanted a kids' show and he had no choice but to give it to them.

"I think Walt had some legitimate concerns," a Disney executive says. "He didn't want to tie up too many of his key people and keep them away from work on films. And, frankly, the speed with which the show had to be done worried him. He was afraid the product might suffer and, in fact, there are still people around here who think it did."

Disney assigned a trusted associate, Bill Walsh, to oversee the show and make sure it came across as a Disney product. His own participation was limited, although, as always, he approved the necessary hirings and firings. Walsh, who began his career writing gags for the Mickey Mouse newspaper strip, had produced the first Disney TV special for the Coca-Cola Company in 1950 and had produced "Disneyland-TV" during its first year. Since television was still in its first decade, Walsh was one of the more experienced producers around.

The heavy organization needed to launch the new series was delegated to Hal Adelquist, who ran the story department. It was Adelquist who was most instrumental in putting the original pieces together and it was Adelquist who was to pay most for the success of the show.

Since the MMC was going to be on for an hour each weekday afternoon and since there was little time for editing or reshooting, the situation obviously called for a director with "live" television experience. Dick (he spelled his name "Dik" in those days) Darley was the logical choice. Darley had been in television since 1948, had launched "Space Patrol" which ran on ABC for five years, and had wide experience with wrestling shows, cooking shows, country and western shows, boxing and used-car commercials. He had also done drama like A *Tale of Two Cities*, "Hollywood Mystery Time," and "Personal Appearance." He was also suited to the job by temperament, being a kind, gentle man whom kids liked immediately.

"The plan," Darley says, "was to shoot with three cameras going at once and then edit the results. Nobody over at Disney had any experience in shooting this way. Not many people anywhere did. I think Lucy may have been using multiple cameras for about a year. But the Disney studio was unique anyway. It was a nice, family operation, not a factory."

With that much shooting going on, things got so crowded that some of the twenty-three-man film-editing crew wound up working in bathrooms. Altogether, the show drew upon the services of over 175 people, not counting performers or musicians.

The concept of the show, which evolved from the creative team that planned it (mainly Walsh, Adelquist, Darley, Jimmie Dodd, and Roy Williams), was relatively simple. The heart of the series was the tremendous backlog of Disney cartoons. The group divided the show into four segments of fifteen minutes each. Undoubtedly, this division had commercial as well as artistic reasons since sponsor time was sold in fifteen-minute blocks. The first segment was "Roll Call" followed by newsreels or Jiminy Cricket; segment two was the major Mouseketeer segment and its format varied from day to day. Segment three was the live-action serials like "Spin & Marty," and segment four featured a cartoon-of-the-day from the Disney library. In addition to their own segment, the Mouseketeers introduced each quarter hour and served to bind the show together.

Things started to get frantic around the studio in the early summer of 1955. With the targeted air date only a few months off, there were still many things to be resolved. What, for example, should the kids wear? Spaceman outfits? Cowboy outfits? Roy Williams, an illustrator who later appeared on the show as the Big Mooseketeer, had come up with an idea they liked. Williams remembered a gag from a 1930 cartoon where Mickey Mouse tipped his hat to Minnie as he passed but instead of a hat, it was

The Merry Mouseketeers as they appeared in late 1956. (Wide World)

California law required performing children to attend school three hours a day. Here, teacher Jean Seaman summons the "red" team to class in the little red trailer on the Disney lot. From left: Annette, Lonnie, Tommy, Darlene, Bobby, Sharon, Doreen, and Karen. (Wide World)

There are no candles on Jimmie Dodd's birthday cake. Jimmie, who looked much younger than he actually was, didn't keep score. Front row: Karen Pendleton, Sharon Baird, Linda Hughes, Cheryl Holdridge, Jimmie, Cubby O'Brien, Johnny Crawford, Don Grady (Agrati). Rear: Roy Williams, Tommy Cole, Bobby Burgess, Ruth Dodd, Bonnie Lynn Fields, Doreen Tracey, and Annette Funicello. (Courtesy Ruth Dodd Braun)

Lonnie Burr, age four and just about to turn pro, hams it up for the camera. (Courtesy Lonnie Burr)

Dallas Johann, the first Mouseketeer hired and the first one fired. Dallas cried whenever the cameras were turned on him and was replaced by his older brother John Lee before the show went on the air. (Courtesy Dallas Johann)

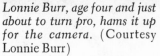

A picture almost too adorable for words. Karen and Cubby introduce the Mousekartoon. (Courtesy Karen Pendleton)

Walter Elias Disney with a drawing of Mickey Mouse in a pose from his original role in Steamboat Willie. *The mouse was first drawn by the brilliant cartoonist Ub Iwerks and while Disney supervised the development of Mickey's personality and adventures, he never could draw him. Disney first wanted to call the creature Mortimer Mouse, but his wife talked him out of it.* (Wide World)

the top of his head. He designed a set of "Mouse" ears based on the gag.

Then, too, there was the Johann kid. Dallas Johann was the first child actor to be hired and Dallas just wasn't working out. He was fine for trying on costumes and things like that but he cried every time anyone turned a camera on him. And some idiot had agreed to pay him $250 a week which was considerably more than the other kids were going to get. Walsh finessed the problem by firing Dallas and hiring his older brother John Lee for the show.

There were other problems, too. Advertisers were beginning to get nervous. Eighteen sponsors had already agreed to put money into a show they had never seen, simply on the basis of its being a Disney product. Altogether, 1,040 commercial quarter hours—$15 million worth—had been sold. But, the Disney people were being awfully secretive about the project. Things got so bad that an ABC executive was forced to sneak the storyboards for the show out of the studio at night, show them to advertisers, and return them the next morning before they were missed.

And, there was an avalanche of kids. Every stage mother within fifty miles of Burbank had responded to the open audition call. The planning team looked at, and listened to, over three thousand kids before settling on the original twenty-four.

The most monumental problem of all, however, belonged to Hal Adelquist. Disney was a man who liked to control projects, to fiddle with things, to get material reshot and redone. Because of the enormous amount of shooting and editing involved in the Mouse Club (one executive later figured it to be the equivalent of six and a half full-length features in a year), there was simply no way that Disney could control the finished product. He took his frustrations out on Adelquist with the result that Adelquist was eventually fired, dropped out of the business, and virtually disappeared. To this day, Disney studio promotional material plays down Adelquist's role in the original conception of the show.

"There was a feeling," says one ex-Disney executive, "that as the show began to come together and began to look like it might be successful, Walt got a little jealous. He was always cool on the subject of the 'Mickey Mouse Club.' He couldn't really afford to like it that much because he hadn't really had that much to do with it."

* * *

The "Mickey Mouse Club" came at a particularly good time for the venerable Mickey. His career had been in a steady decline since the war. He was still a great marketing symbol, of course, but he had begun to take himself seriously and had grown into a straight man for Donald Duck and Goofy, both of whom had become stars.

Like the man who created him, Mickey had become more conservative, better behaved, no longer irascible. He was also less lovable. When the always foul-tempered Donald interrupted the opening of the Mouse Club screaming "Donald Duck" at the top of his lungs, he was raising a valid point. At the time, he was a bigger star.

There seems to be little question that Walt preferred Mickey to the rest of the cartoon gang. He was, after all, Mickey's voice and the Mouse mirrored Disney's own thoughts and actions. As Uncle Walt became more settled and prosperous, so did Mickey.

Actually, there might never have been a Mickey Mouse were it not for a Universal executive named Charles Mintz. In the late 1920s, Disney had created a character named Oswald the Rabbit and Universal was distributing those cartoons. Mintz figured he could cut production costs by simply stealing Oswald and hiring Disney's illustrators.

It was a valuable lesson for the young Disney. No one ever took him in business again. His response to Mintz was to create—and copyright—Mickey Mouse. The rest, as they say, is history.

The legacy of the Mintz incident resides with Walt Disney Productions even today. Among writers who need access to photographs and materials to do their work, there is general agreement that Disney is the least co-operative, most openly paranoid studio in Hollywood. Lawyers for the studio pursue trivial infringement matters to absurd ends. It's a shame, really, because it makes writing even nice things about the studio difficult.

Disney stopped making cartoon shorts in 1956, a year after the Mouse Club began. His cartoons were taking a drubbing anyway from Warner Brothers' "Looneytunes" which were—if not as technically well done—much faster paced and funnier. The decision was made to concentrate on live-action and full-length cartoon features.

It is interesting that Disney could never draw Mickey Mouse. Roy Williams frequently taught ten-year-old children to draw Mickey in less than a minute. Walt, although he could draw a little, could never get the little rascal right. A shrink could probably make something of that.

* * *

With the exception of Bobby Burgess, who was from Long Beach, they were all Valley kids. Their fathers were laborers, meatcutters, filling-station operators, truck drivers, and carpenters. Their common bond was that they had all had dance or music lessons. That's how they had been found.

When Bill Walsh began scouring the area for child performers, he enlisted the aid of Burch Mann Holtzman, a dance instructress who operated a studio. She, in turn, put the word out to the other dance studios. Disney is looking for kids who can sing and dance and have a nice personality.

And the kids they found did have personalities, separate and distinct. Annette and Sharon Baird were sunny, easygoing, and cooperative. Bobby Burgess smiled so much that the other kids suspected he was a phony. Darlene Gillespie, older than the other girls, was aloof and standoffish. She, more than any of the others, had some comprehension of what was going on around her. Cubby and Karen were babies really; Karen more than Cubby. Doreen was a natural clown, radiant with her saucer-shaped eyes and budding sexiness. Tommy was too nice to be believed. Lonnie was cocky and professional, a sharp dresser, and a smart kid. When Cheryl joined the group a year later, she was something of a mystery girl. Her father had been a general in the Army, a fact that put her into a slightly different class.

For the most part, they were just average kids. "Don't get me those kind with the tightly curled hairdos—tap dancers—get me children who look like they're having fun. Then later we can teach them to tap dance or sing or whatever," Walt Disney reportedly told Walsh.

Lonnie and Sharon were professionals, though, and Bobby and Tommy had both appeared in enough talent contests to qualify as professionals. The rest were just kids.

They got on well with each other, for the most part. The Disney organization kept a close watch on the behavior of its charges. If a kid was a troublemaker, he was out at the end of his thirteen-week-option period.

There was the usual fooling around, of course. Dennis Day, who grew up to become something of a hippie, once found some stage blood and smeared it all over his arm. He ran up to Darlene writhing in agony only to notice, too late, that she was talking to Uncle Walt. Disney was not amused.

Walsh worked out most of the social problems in a masterful way. He divided the twenty-four regulars into three teams—the "red," "white," and "blue." The "red" team kids were really the stars. They got to say their names on "Roll Call" and were more prominently featured in all the segments.

Ironically, several of the "blue" and "white" team Mouseketeers have shown more show business staying power than most of the members of the "red" team. Don Agrati changed his name to Don Grady and became one of the stars of "My Three Sons" (he's since changed it back and made a record or two); Sherry Allen went back to her old name, Sherry Alberoni, and at twenty-eight is one of Hollywood's brighter young actresses, having appeared among other things as Jody's girlfriend on the soap opera "Bright Promise"; Johnny Crawford played Chuck Connors' son on "The Rifleman" and recently starred in *The Naked Ape*; Dickie Dodd sang with a rock group called The Standells which had a couple of hits; Bonnie Lynn Fields became a splendid and busy dancer; Paul Peterson is a writer, and Lynn Ready had a recording contract with Motown.

"We really didn't have a lot of contact with the red team people," says John Lee Johann, now a New York actor. "Naturally we didn't get as much mail because we weren't featured. In a way, I guess we were extras for the red team. We filmed while they went to school and they did their segments while we were in class."

California law requires that performing children attend class three hours a day but the hours need not be consecutive. When Walsh finished with one batch and was set up for another production number, he would simply walk over to the little red trailer on the studio lot and retrieve the kids he needed for the shot and send the others back to class.

He handled one potential problem before it had a chance to become one. California law also requires that performing children be accompanied by an adult, in the most of the Mouseketeers' instances, their mother. Walsh converted a screening room into a sort of ladies lounge with a TV set and a sewing machine. The parents spent their days there. They were strictly barred from the set.

This didn't totally prevent some parents from getting involved in the ongoing activities on the set. John Johann remembers being waylaid on his way to the set one day by "Hack" O'Brien who offered to give him a short lesson in drumming. John says he told him he had to go for a shot and was told that they wouldn't be ready for several minutes. When Johann finally made it to the set he discovered that the scene had already been shot and that Walsh had used Cubby instead.

Johann also remembers starting a little rumor about having seen Annette kiss Bobby behind the red trailer and finding himself being publicly dressed down by Annette's mother in the cafeteria.

Several of the kids detected an overly friendly attitude between one of the casting directors and the mother of one particularly cute little Mouse.

The kids, themselves, worked well together. Most of the temper tantrums were directed, for some reason or another, at Bobby. Once Bonnie Kern, angry at Bobby over some slight, chose a moment when he was lifting her over his head during a dance number to spit on him.

There were the little romances that are inevitable among impressionable young kids. Annette and Lonnie were a number for a while, a combination of which her father, Joe, strongly disapproved. Karen and Cubby were an inevitable couple, as were Bobby and Sharon since they always danced together.

They were model children, for the most part, envisioned in the great Disney oversimplification as representative of all American children of the era. The Disney public relations department, so impressed by the manifest destiny of its wards and so confident of the show's role in shaping the future, was even moved to the hyperbole: "The 'Mickey Mouse Club' is dedicated to the leaders of the twenty-first century, some of whom are among you Mouseketeers of today. The skills and arts and sciences which you are developing will help fashion a better world for tomorrow. Everyone of us has some talent and talent is developed by doing. This is the theme of our television show."

*   *   *

There was no news film of the space launch. Only an image on the rear-screen projector behind David Brinkley's head. It was an ugly little monster . . . a pumpkin with antennas. The Russians called it Sputnik and they proudly announced it to the world as evidence of their educational superiority over the Americans.

I was shocked by the news. How could a country as primitive and backward as the Soviet Union pull off such an enormous technological achievement as the breaking of the barrier of space? Were we not the greatest country in the world, after all? Had I been lied to all these years?

There was a scandal in the educational establishment, hand wringing, shakeups, weeping, and gnashing of teeth. Johnny couldn't read. He sure as hell couldn't read a slide rule.

Suddenly, people like Dr. Max Rafferty, head of California's school system, the man who once said that "Disney is the greatest educator of the century," began to look even more foolish.

There was work to be done, obviously. Exceptional students, even those who were merely average, began to feel the subtle pressures to study science. Hundreds who might have become artists or poets became instead engineers. NASA was born. We had to catch the Russians at any cost.

The great national wave of paranoia spread even to the small country school where I went. A science teacher was added. Those with an interest in science were tested, coddled, prodded. The space race was on.

Other chinks began to appear in the armor of smug insomnia that had engulfed the nation. People marched in Little Rock and Birmingham, disc jockeys admitted that they took money for playing certain records, a man named Charles Van Doren, son of a famous intellectual, admitted that he was given answers in advance on a quiz show.

Out in Nebraska, Charles Starkweather and his teen-age girlfriend, Caril Ann Fugate, went on a senseless murder spree that left eleven people dead. Starkweather was fried in the Nebraska electric chair in 1959. Caril Ann—who is the same age as Annette Funicello—was paroled this year.

* * *

The casting of the adult roles for the show was often done in an oblique manner. Jimmie Dodd, a journeyman bit player in films and a composer with steady, if somewhat modest, abilities, had been hired to write music for the Mouse Club. Adelquist and Walsh heard him singing and felt he would make an excellent emcee for the show. Their problem was how to convince Walt. Disney was not very involved in the preparations for the show and he was surly on the subject. He was particularly surly about Adelquist who was displaying a lot of take-charge initiative with regard to the MMC. He was not likely to be amenable to a suggestion from the young upstart.

Walsh and Adelquist called Disney in, under the pretext of

hearing some new material for the show. Jimmie sang and played several of his songs.

"Hey," Disney said, after listening for a few minutes, "why don't we have Jimmie perform on the show?" Everybody agreed that Walt had a terrific idea there.

The "Mickey Mouse Club" premiered on October 3, 1955. It was an immediate hit in the ratings. ABC gleefully reported that it was the highest rated daytime television show "of all time." *Billboard* found that in eight of the ten cities it polled regularly, the show led all others. Another network simply gave the time back to its affiliates rather than buck the ratings.

The critics were considerably less charitable. Jack Gould, writing in the October 4 issue of the New York *Times* said:

> Walt Disney's long-awaited afternoon show for children . . . had its premiere yesterday on Channel 7. Hopeful parents who had assumed that Mr. Disney would bring about a long-needed revolution in adolescent TV programming, can only keep their fingers crossed. His debut bordered on the disastrous.
>
> Not only was the opening show roughly on a par with any number of existing displays of juvenile precocity, but Mr. Disney and the American Broadcasting Company went commercial to a degree almost without precedent.
>
> In the sixty minutes between 5 and 6 o'clock there were twenty commercials, one of which burst smack in the middle of a "Pluto" cartoon. This viewer cannot recall ever having seen a children's program—or an adult's for that matter—that was as commercial as Mr. Disney's which easily is the new season's most distressing news. Apparently even a contemporary genius is not immune to the virus of video.

John Crosby, writing in the New York *Herald-Tribune*, was not any more kind:

> When my children say the program is always telling them what to do I think they mean by that they are incessantly

being asked to go buy something. . . . Our children are asked to buy Mickey Mouse dolls, Sugar Jets, burp guns and heaven knows what else on the average of every four minutes.

Now, kids, as I guess we all know, seem to enjoy commercials. But to spray plugs at a child in this quantity amounts to —if I read my child's mind at all correctly—a form of nagging. Get this. Get that. A child can take only so much—and this is too much.

By the end of year one, Walt Disney felt the show needed change. Adelquist was demoted to scout for talent for the "Talent Round-Up" segment. Sidney Miller replaced Dick Darley as director of the show.

Miller knew a lot about kid actors. He had been one, himself, beginning on stage in New York with *The Children's Hour* and *The Lady Next Door*. When he was fourteen, his parents moved him to the Coast for the greater opportunity. He was in *Penrod and Son* and *Boy's Town*. He knew Judy and Mickey and Donald and worked with them all. He and O'Connor became close friends and even did a Vegas act together. Nowadays, he divides his time almost equally between acting, directing, and writing.

He was a tough taskmaster. All of the kids were asked to audition again. He was, and is, a funny man and he got the kids to do what he wanted. It didn't help much, though.

Despite the show's enormous first-season ratings, sponsors started falling off in the second year and by the beginning of the third season, in 1957, the format had been trimmed down to a half hour. "Answer to the sales resistance, according to ABC-TV, is that there are only a limited amount of bankrollers for a kiddie program," *Variety* reported. "Of course, another explanation may be that the novelty of 'Mickey Mouse' may have worn off."

ence. During a story conference for the Mouse Club, Hal
Adelquist was outlining a sequence called "How to Ride a Bicy-
cle." "Now when you get on your bicycle—" Adelquist began.
Walt interrupted. "Change *your* bicycle to *a* bicycle," he said.
"Not every kid is fortunate enough to have a bike of his own."

Although he wove his daydreams with the aid of others, Disney
was essentially a loner, a man who listened only to his own
drummer. He was a self-made man, an incurable romantic, a man
of destiny. He was one of the truly, organically, American breed.
Secretary of State Henry Kissinger once said in an interview: "I've
always acted alone. Americans admire that enormously. Americans admire the cowboy leading the caravan alone astride his
horse, the cowboy entering a village or city alone on his horse.
Without even a pistol, maybe, because he doesn't go in for shooting. He acts, that's all: aiming at the right spot at the right time.
A Wild West tale, if you like. . . . This romantic, surprising
character suits me, because being alone has always been part of
my style, or of my technique, if you prefer. Independence too.
Yes, that's very important to me and in me. And, finally, convic-
tion. I am always convinced of the necessity of whatever I'm
doing. And people feel that, believe in it."

Kissinger, in describing himself, described Disney perfectly.

The "Mickey Mouse Club" was a better show than it might
have been expected to be. It was better because it represented, in
many ways, the concerns of Bill Walsh, Hal Adelquist, and Jimmie Dodd. It was less than it might have been because they were
forced to work under the umbrella of the Disney philosophy.

The Club was a bittersweet blend of innocence and commercial hyperbole and it had an enormous influence on what the
kids who watched it thought or, at least, believed they should
think. Part of its impact is probably due to the fact that it came
early in television's history, that it reached a generation of video
virgins, so to speak. Television is a separate reality (Daniel Ells-
berg once said that he only became aware of the brutality of the
Vietnam war after he came back from Vietnam and began watching the news on television) and one gains experience in it the
more one watches. Many kids today consider the "Mickey Mouse

Club" too unsophisticated, too cornball, for serious consideration.

Another part of the show's impact had to do with its really not being a children's show at all but, rather, a show that featured children playing the roles of little adults. All of the values the show taught—reliability, reverence, bravery, loyalty, good behavior, the icky-sticky grown-up concept of romantic love—are things that adults think kids should be taught.

Unlike its newfangled successors—"Sesame Street" and the "Electric Company"—the Mouse Club did not attempt to teach mechanical skills like reading, writing, and spelling. The educational emphasis of the MMC was morality, as Walt Disney and those who worked for him, perceived it. What the Club wanted to instill was nothing less than a philosophy of life, a picture of the ideal world. And, at the time—incredibly only twenty years ago—that philosophy seemed reasonable and viable enough. You can be whatever you want to be if only you have faith and work hard toward that goal. You can truly know what is right and what is wrong.

In this light, the "Mickey Mouse Club" was no less an important instrument of national policy than the most flagrant propaganda of *Pravda*. To fourteen million children daily, the Club promised a better and brighter world in the future. The Club sold stock in a glamour company that has since fallen off the Big Board. Its shareholders—its believers—are disillusioned and estranged.

*   *   *

The "Mickey Mouse Club" was not an original idea in 1955. The concept was born in 1931, a few years after Mickey Mouse began to conquer the world with his cartoons and merchandise. With the guidance of the Disneys—Walt and Roy—theater owners across the nation began organizing "Mickey Mouse Clubs" as a promotion for their theaters. It was a way of bringing kids into theaters on Saturday mornings. Some of the Clubs organized bands and, as a matter of fact, Disney's future ace animator, Ward Kimball, once played in one.

The Disney organization, anxious to do its part to promote the

Mickey pictures, supported the theater owners' efforts by issuing a newspaper for Club members called the *Official Bulletin of the Mickey Mouse Club* with Lucille Allen Benedict as general manager.

Dave Smith, who runs the Disney archives in Burbank, gave me a copy of the April 1, 1932, issue of the *Bulletin* and it has such headlines as "Juneau Club Publishes Its Own Paper" and "Celebrate Kindness to Animals Week April 16th." The paper also had a story promoting the latest Mickey Mouse epic which was called "Barnyard Olympics" and a report that twenty-five new Mickey Mouse Clubs had opened in Chicago. One of the most intriguing items read as follows:

> He may be "His Honor, the Mayor of Des Moines" to you but he's just a Mickey Mouse to hundreds of boys and girls of Des Moines.

> At the conclusion of a talk on George Washington, given before the Mickey Mouse Club in the Des Moines Theatre recently, Mayor Parker Crouch of that city was initiated into the Club as "honorary" chief Mickey Mouse.

Presumably, the expression "Mickey Mouse" had not yet acquired the pejorative meaning it now has. While often descriptive of the state of latter-day politics, it seems unlikely that any politician today would want to take it on.

The most enlightening part of the *Bulletin* are the homilies sprinkled throughout under the heading "Vagrant Philosophies of Uncle Churchmouse." They are revealing about what has come to be known as the Disney philosophy and are likely antecedents to Jimmie Dodd's "Doddisms." Here are just a few:

> After all, the canny, cautious, thrifty and suspicious people form the bulwark of modern civilization.

> Side-walks along crowded city streets will move in the future; roofs will be used far more than at present; needless noise will be abolished.

> Few young folks are judged by the actual results they accomplish; but if they are inspired by a devotion to duty and a

love of hard work, they make a powerful impression on employers just the same.

* * *

The "Mickey Mouse Club" ended its network run after the 1957 season. Advertisers have given up on the show but in 1962 there was a resurgence of interest and the Disney organization put the Club into syndication. By then, over half a million Mickey Mouse hats—designed by Roy Williams—had been sold. The figure now is close to two million. Over seventy-five manufacturers had brought out products related to the MMC.

There are many who believe that the end of the network run had more to do with squabbles between the Disneys and ABC than a lack of advertisers.

The dispute centered on two fronts. When ABC agreed to lend Disney money to finance the completion of Disneyland, they acquired the rights to all the food concessions at the park, except those held by Swift & Company. The Disneys have always been infamous for taking on partners when they need cash and dumping them later when things get rosier. By 1959, Disneyland was beginning to look immensely profitable and Roy Disney launched a backbiting campaign against ABC. "Those people don't know how to run concessions," he was fond of saying. "I wish we had it." Roy was assisted in his campaign by his number one yes-man, Card Walker, a former messenger boy who now runs Walt Disney Productions.

"The Disneys are incredible," says one former ABC executive. "They'll get in bed with you but later, when they're finished, they kick you out."

Disney's other complaint against ABC was more legitimate. ABC has always been the weak sister network and, in those days, it was even more so. ABC simply had weak "clearance." For example, when Danny Thomas jumped ABC for CBS, the number of stations his show was seen on went from 90 to 195 immediately. Things were so bad that the Disneys had to make additional 16mm "bicycle" prints of both the Mouse Club and "Disneyland-

TV" which were shipped from station to station in some regions of the country as much as a week after their original broadcast date.

The major obstacle that the Roy Disney-Card Walker faction had to overcome was Walt who had a particular fondness for Bob Kintner, then president of ABC. But Kintner himself went to NBC and the Disneys went with him. They settled the broadcasting and park loans with ABC for $7.5 million.

When Disney reissued the "Mickey Mouse Club" in syndication in 1962, it had a line-up of 119 stations. The show ran in syndication in the United States through 1965. When it was canceled, the show still had nearly ten million viewers.

* * *

The idea for this book grew out of a certain malaise I felt a couple of years ago. I was going to be thirty and the thought struck me that a lot of people my age were unhappy. They did strange things like become Buddhists or bought farms in the Berkshires.

The subject of anomie fascinated me. I began clipping articles about odd behavior by my contemporaries. A thirty-year-old curator at the Whitney Museum killed himself. A thirty-year-old television broadcaster in Florida blew her head off during a newscast. An all-pro guard for the Dallas Cowboys went berserk and tried to rip down the door of a rabbi's house.

The best one though was about a thirty-year-old businessman in St. Louis named David Hanley. What Hanley had done was drive a new Cadillac El Dorado into the landing gear of American Airlines Flight 119 as it prepared to take off in St. Louis. He did this in an attempt to stop a hijacking that was in progress.

I got an assignment from *Esquire* and went to see Hanley. He was, I swear, as normal as you or me.

On the way out of Hanley's house, I asked him—for no particular reason—if he had ever watched the "Mickey Mouse Club."

"Sure," he said. "I had the ears and everything. I wish my kids could see that kind of show now instead of the trash that's on. That's a show that taught real values."

3

Annette—
The Mouse Princess
and the Beginning

Annette is still an unlikely fantasy. Annette Funicello, dream girl of the fifties, first love to a generation, a breathing reincarnation of malt shops, sock hops, penny loafers, pony tails, and slumber parties, sits in a high-backed wicker chair sipping scotch and smoking a Lark on an ordinary afternoon in Encino.

"Is it two o'clock yet?" she says. "My daughter gets home from school about two."

She is a beautiful child-woman. The afternoon California sun filters through the drapes behind, casting pools of light on her dark brunette hair and accentuating her porcelainlike face and oversized eyes. She seems, at this moment, a perfect product of an artistic union of Botticelli and Walter Keene. The innocence has returned. American International nearly destroyed that forever with those beach party pictures in which Annette came across as a fat, disingenuous little creature with horribly teased Freda's

Beauty Shoppe hair and skin that never tanned. What we have here is an older, more mature Annette, who, at thirty-two, seems to have regained that peculiar charm that dazzled fourteen million kids daily on the "Mickey Mouse Club."

"The Mouse Club was the happiest time of my life," she says. "I know people think this is goody-goody. They say 'Annette, you're sugar-coating it. It couldn't have been that good.' But, it really was the happiest days of my life."

She means it, too. Annette is nothing if not sincere. To understand just what she meant to her generation, you have to go back a bit and pick up a little history.

Joe and Virginia Funicello moved their family out from Utica, New York, in 1947, settling in Studio City where Joe opened a filling station and garage. The Funicellos were, and still are, a close-knit Italian family fond of get-togethers and food and just being alive. They had two boys, Joey and Mike, and a pretty, dark-eyed little girl named Annette.

Annette was a polite, pampered, enthusiastic, happy child of modest talents and slightly above-average academic potential. She wanted, as many little girls did at that time, to be a ballerina. She took dance lessons.

Walt Disney saw her dancing at the Burbank Starlight Bowl one night and asked her dance teacher to bring her in to audition for the "Mickey Mouse Club." It was to be his major contribution to the show. At this point, producers Bill Walsh and Hal Adelquist and host Jimmie Dodd had already looked at nearly three thousand kids and selected twenty-three. Nobody was overwhelmed by Annette's talent potential but she was cute and she was the boss's suggestion. She was hired, mainly to make it an even twenty-four Mouseketeers, and assigned to the blue, or second team.

"I worshiped Mr. Disney," Annette says. "I loved everything he stood for. I could see his love for children. I found him very shy. If there was a member of the crew who said 'damn' or 'hell,' he was gone the next day. He was so protective of the kids."

Annette smiles. Sweetly. She means it, too.

*   *   *

The "Mickey Mouse Club" premiered on ABC on October 3, 1955, and became an immediate sensation with the kids, although critics were cool. The Funicello kid, particularly, worked out better than anybody could have imagined.

"Until the mail started coming in," one studio exec recalls, "everybody in the studio expected someone like Cubby O'Brien to steal the show.

"Annette was the last person anybody at Disney's or ABC would have picked. She had a nice smile and a sweet personality and that was all. She lacked the talent for the elaborate routines all those kids on the first team were chosen for."

But, by the end of the first week the series was on the air, the mail response was such that Annette was promoted to the red team and was on her way to becoming a genuine 1950s-style legend.

The irony, of course, is that Annette really was the least-talented first-string Mouseketeer (with the exception of Karen Pendleton who just happened to be little and cute). Bobby Burgess, Lonnie Burr, and Sharon Baird were better dancers; Darlene Gillespie could sing much better. But Annette . . . wow, Annette had that certain magic something of which stars are made.

Just what that something was, exactly, nobody ever quite figured out. But it quickly became obvious to all that Annette was *the* star of the show. Within a few weeks she was getting close to four thousand letters a month, nearly one third of the total for the entire cast.

One cynical ex-Mouse maintains that it was because Annette had lots of relatives, which is possible, although it seems unlikely that any family is dedicated enough to write that many letters.

A former viewer says Annette's appeal was due to the fact that she was precociously developed, but the fact of the matter is, Doreen Tracy and Bonnie Kern were much more, you know, *physical*.

What Annette Funicello had (and this is the basis of her peculiar magic) were the qualities of honesty, sweetness, spirituality, and, alas, virginity that most typified the aspirations and presumed moral ambiance of that era. She was the absolute perfect embodiment of the 1950s ideal—the girl next door whom you would never try to get to go all the way because she was a good girl and you wanted to marry her someday and make babies.

Disney quickly recognized Annette's enormous capacity to stir the awakening fantasies of a generation of twelve-year-olds. It was all there in those moist letters that poured in by the thousands. Annette was hot; she was a property that could be sold and, miracle of miracles, she needed almost no packaging. She was exactly what she appeared to be. Her on-screen and off-screen personalities were, and are, the same. Disney was always protective of Annette's image and several years later it was he who persuaded her not to wear a bikini in those beach pictures but to opt for a modest one-piece instead.

At the time, though, Disney was publicly coy about the idea of having "stars" on the show. "These are just regular American kids," his press people were fond of quoting him as saying. "There isn't a show-off among them. Perhaps the most remarkable feature of the Mouseketeers is their refreshing normalcy. When they are not dressed for the show, you can't tell them from any of your neighborhood small fry."

Not surprisingly, though, Annette began getting more to do. She was cast in the "Spin & Marty" serial with Tim Considine and David Stollery, a light teen-age romantic role which played to her fantasy image. With the encouragement of the American Dairy Association, she and Sammy Ogg went for a two-week visit to a dairy farm to film something called "The Dairy Story."

There was a good deal of friction between Annette and Darlene Gillespie and their two families. Darlene was almost the exact opposite of Annette. She was a born cynic, she was talented, and she was a freckle-faced kid who was not very pretty. Her own series "Corky and the White Shadow" with Buddy Ebsen had failed to generate the kind of response that Annette had stirred in "Spin

& Marty." Everyone who knew her agrees that Darlene, even as a kid, was a smart, tough cookie. What she had going for her was one of the most moving and beautiful voices of any child actress ever to move through Hollywood. The Disney studio made wide use of her voice and you can buy her recordings of songs from *Snow White* and *Cinderella* to this day.

After the Mouse Club stopped shooting, Annette was kept under contract by the studio and all the other Mouseketeers, Darlene included, were let go. It was a real irony because Darlene was supergifted. But Annette was something more. She was a star.

And, of course, stars get most of the breaks. Bill Walsh, who used to come over to Annette's parents' house every Christmas Eve for home-cooked Italian food, wrote a song for the Annette series called "How Will I Know My Love?" People began writing in for it, so Annette recorded it. The record sold half a million copies. She followed up with two smash hits "Tall Paul" and "First Name Initial."

Although Annette was clearly Uncle Walt's favorite, not everything was entirely rosy at the studio as an item in the December 18, 1959, edition of the Los Angeles *Times* indicates:

"Annette Funicello, 17-year-old singer, yesterday made a futile attempt to have Superior Judge Benjamin Landis set aside the 1955 court approval of her seven-year contract with Disney Productions, Inc.

"Judge Landis, as he dismissed her motion, held with Atty. Spencer C. Olin for Disney that the court had no jurisdiction to set aside its own approval of the agreement.

"Miss Funicello, whose current record, 'First Name Initial,' is among the top 10 hits, complained that the pact was inequitable and that she was without an agent or legal counsel when she signed it.

"She was represented in the petition by Atty. Harvey Grossman.

"The agreement started with $160 weekly salary and rose by option to a present $325. It will graduate in 1962 to $500 if all options are exercised."

The Disney victory was brief, however, because a year later Annette was back in court and this time it was she who won. Her salary was raised immediately to $500 a week with regular increases up to $1,050 a week at the end of four years. She was also guaranteed forty weeks employment a year, with permission to make personal appearances and outside engagements.

Altogether, during her nine years under contract to Disney, Annette earned a quarter of a million dollars. Her court-ordered savings—20 per cent of the total—amounted to $49,950.

When asked what she planned to do with the money, the Los Angeles *Times* reported: "First get my folks a new car," she bubbled ecstatically. "Then buy myself some clo-o-thes." The article went on to say: "County Trust and Revenue Officer Benjamin K. Cheny said he couldn't remember a larger fund put aside for a juvenile player, mouseketeer or otherwise."

On January 9, 1965, at the age of twenty-two, Annette married her agent, Jack Gilardi, a lean, good-looking square shooter she had first met when she was fourteen on the set of *Babes in Toyland*. Gilardi works for International Creative Management, a giant talent agency. He had dated Annette for eight months before the wedding.

It was the kind of ceremony you always thought it would be. Annette was radiant in a Chantilly lace filmy sheath with a long cathedral train. Over a thousand people jammed St. Cyril's Roman Catholic Church for the long, long noon mass. Annette's mother, Virginia, was frantic. Lots of relatives. Lots of crying. It was all very schmaltzy and beautiful.

The reception for a mere five hundred fifty got underway at seven at the Beverly Hilton. Two orchestras took turns as other newlyweds like Nancy Sinatra and Tommy Sands unleashed the Watusi, the dance rage of the moment. Another orchestra, Murray Korda's, came up from the Monseigneur Room for Annette and Jack's grand entrance. The Gilardis came in under an arch of violin bows as the Korda band broke into the "Mickey Mouse Club" theme. Annette and Jack left the party at eleven but returned shortly and stayed until closing.

"As for the bride," wrote Mike Connolly in the *Hollywood Reporter*, "you are so right, Charlie Brown—she has grown up to be so beautiful, we feel like we're losing money every minute we waste not writing her up for *Vogue*."

But, alas, her marriage was the beginning of the end of Annette, the performer. Although she has made a couple of pictures since, her professional career has been pretty much confined to being spokeswoman for Mennen baby products and head bat girl for the Dodger All-Star Game.

"Jack is so protective of Annette," offered a friend of the family. "He shields her from any unpleasantness. Like, remember when Johnny Carson was doing a running series of Annette Funicello jokes, I don't think she ever knew about that. Annette has had a very sheltered life. She went from a protective family to a protective studio to a protective marriage. She's really never had a chance to grow on her own or to become what she truly has the capacity to be. I'm not sure it's a good thing."

In any event, Annette has shown little independence publicly.

"When I have babies," Annette said, right after her marriage, "I don't want them brought up by a nurse. I'll either quit the movies entirely or limit my pictures to one a year."

Unlike the thousand other starlets who have taken the pledge, Annette really meant it.

Talent Round-Up time for the gang. From left: Eileen Diamond, Jimmie, Sharon, Jay Jay Solari, and Cubby. (UPI)

Jimmie goes over some music with Sidney Miller, who directed the show in its second season. (Wide World)

Jimmie gives Cubby a lift at his eleventh birthday party in Hollywood. Millions of kids learned about right and wrong from Jimmie Dodd. (Wide World)

Fun-loving Roy Williams and reverent Jimmie Dodd were an unlikely pair but they got along well together. (UPI)

"God wants some of us to become scientists, some of us to become artists, some of us to become firemen and doctors and trapeze artists. And He gives each of us the special talents to become these things, provided we work to develop them. . . . So: Know Thyself. Learn to understand your talents and then work to develop them. That's the way to be happy." *Jimmie Dodd, 1955* (UPI)

The late Roy Disney at Disney World in Orlando, Florida. Roy ran the corporate side of Walt Disney Productions and was crucial to its commercial growth. Money he and Walt had saved enabled Mickey Mouse to have a voice in Steamboat Willie, *released in the early days of talkies. (UPI)*

4

Lonnie—
Notes on Rebellion

The beginning is a preamble. Back in the good old days, about 1957 or so, a survey was conducted among high school students in Oklahoma and it produced some truly enlightening results. When asked what person they would most like to be, a majority of the boys polled named either Pat Boone, Ricky Nelson, or President Eisenhower. Most of the girls answered Debbie Reynolds, Elizabeth Taylor, or Natalie Wood.

There is little cause to hope that a national survey would have produced much different results. Nor is it surprising that when our present-day nostalgia merchants began recycling the "fab fifties" they focused their efforts on the kind of bubble-gum madness reflected in that study.

But believe it or not, boys and girls, there was another dimension to the fifties. The other, admittedly minority, viewpoint was represented by an uneasy coalition of intellectual kids—those who were discovering Alan Watts and Kerouac and Camus—and the wild ones—those who drank Bud from the bottle and drove too fast, the boys who turned their collars up and fancied themselves

James Dean; the girls who let you feel them up in study hall; the angries like Charlie Starkweather who carried their resentment on their sleeves and eventually exploded into rifts of senseless violence.

And, of course, there was Elvis. Elvis was the ultimate rebel symbol of his decade, a genital-focused center of a gathering discontent. Middle-class mothers hated Elvis because he threatened their daughters; he exuded the kind of scary sexuality—rape fear— that they had only associated with black men. Forget that off-stage Elvis was always the complete gentleman toward women, he was free with his body and that freedom was frightening.

Lonnie Burr was different from the other Mouseketeers, somehow. He was both an intellectual and a rebel. He seemed more grown-up, was interested in what we folks on the East Coast like to call "the arts," and never used a one-syllable word if a two-syllable word would do. An experienced performer and protégé of dancer Louis de Pron, he was also something of a cynic—the kind of kid who wouldn't be caught dead watching a dumb program like the "Mickey Mouse Club." Because he always seemed to have money and wear good clothes, most of the other kids thought he was rich. Oddly enough, several still think so.

In truth, Lonnie's background was not that far removed from the lower-middle-class beginnings of most of the Mouseketeers. Born Leonard Burr Babin in Newport, Kentucky, on May 31, 1943, his parents—once a vaudeville team known as "Dot and Dash,"—moved out to the Coast in 1946. Howard Babin was by then a truck driver and Lonnie's mother, Dorothy, in the process of taking her young son around, became an agent.

Lonnie's grandparents moved to California a couple of years later and it was they—more than his parents—who were the source of his seeming good fortune. The elder Burrs opened a furniture store, one of the first maple shops on the Coast, in Pasadena, right there on Colorado Avenue where each year the "Parade of Roses" goes by. They were most successful in a Mom-and-Pop entrepreneurial sort of way. His mother is now married to the bar manager of the Stardust and lives in Las Vegas. He seldom sees his father who is still in Los Angeles.

"He's a simple, upright, direct sort of guy," Lonnie says. "He must be sixty-two or so now and is in better shape than I am. He loves to go dancing and has absolutely no gut. I hope I hold up that well."

Lonnie has a good-natured, blond Germanic look about him, although to be sure his hair is thinning a bit these days. He is still extremely clothes-conscious, wears oversized glasses, and his total image seems fixed in a transitional phase, somewhere between Hollywood actor and New York playwright.

Until he moved back to L.A. last year, Lonnie lived in New York, on the Upper West Side, with a girlfriend in one of those newfangled arrangements of which Mr. Disney would almost certainly have disapproved. I saw him rather frequently. When he was between acting gigs, which was frequently, he sometimes did some straight work as a production assistant for a petroleum association not far from my office in midtown Manhattan and we had lunch together. I like him a lot.

If the Mouseketeers could be said to have had an intellectual in their group, Lonnie is it. He graduated from high school at fourteen, earned a B.A. from San Fernando State (now the University of California at Northridge) at eighteen, and later got a master's degree in theater arts from UCLA. He is the only red team Mouseketeer with an advanced degree, although Bobby Burgess is only a few credits away. Lonnie has written a couple of plays (one, called *The Quality of Mercy Is Not Strained*, was produced at UCLA), an unpublished and not half-bad novel, and contributes poems regularly to the "little" magazines.

One of the things that Lonnie is not is an ardent Walt Disney fan.

"Disney didn't give a damn about content," he tells me one day over lunch. "His whole *modus operandi* was making money. True, he had this middle-class Calvinistic idea of good and bad. But then it got to the point of not mattering what was good or bad but rather presenting what people believed was good. So you have animals that don't go to the bathroom. It's a false picture of life. It all comes out to be a nice place where pansies grow and there are no snakes. I find it just morally reprehensible.

"I think the values he used in *Snow White*, in the Mouse Club, in *Chitty Chitty Bang Bang* are drek. I must confess that I do like *Fantasia* though."

Because Lonnie is outspoken, competitive, and comes into every conversation prepared to do battle, I often used him as a sounding board for ideas about the Mouseketeers or to test certain stories. One day I asked Lonnie if it were true, as Annette had told me, that stagehands who said damn or hell in front of the children were fired.

"That is a blatant, out-and-out canard," Lonnie says. "It just isn't true." (Actually, I had my doubts about that one, too. Once when Dick, then Dik, Darley came on the set he was greeted by a sign that said "DIK Is a PRK.")

Lonnie and Annette used to be close and, in fact, were probably the first puppy-love romance to blossom on the Mouseketeer set. I tried out my notion that Annette had special qualities that made her the most popular of the Mouseketeers.

"I disagree with you," he says. "I don't think she had any particular magic. What she had was exposure. She lucked out right at the beginning of the media-created star.

"I don't know if this is true or not. It may just be conjecture but there was a rumor going around that Annette had written to all her relatives and they, in turn, had written to other people, so pretty soon everybody was writing in to the show and she began getting more parts. The world, you have to remember, was a very different place in 1955 and the Disney people tended to measure things in terms of mail response.

"I mean, if Annette had all that response and it was legitimate, why hasn't she ever gone anywhere? She's done an amazing lot of films; she's been on TV specials and talk shows and nothing important has ever happened to her."

Lonnie, who was a busy child performer in the early 1950s, having done—among many other things—thirteen appearances on the

"Colgate Comedy Hour," isn't quite sure how he wound up being a Mouseketeer. He suspects the worst, however.

"My mother told me this story—and she has no reason to lie about it—that the casting director at Disney threatened to have her, and me, blackballed if I didn't sign for the show. I have no firsthand knowledge of that and you must remember that everything I tell you is how I perceived it as a child. But it was very strange.

"I was getting a lot of work and making a good bit of money at the time and I was up for some very good parts. I tested against Johnny Washbrook for "My Friend Flicka." Obviously, it would have been better to be making $750 a week instead of the pittance they were paying at Disney."

At any rate, Lonnie became a Mouseketeer. It wasn't a role that he carried with much genuine enthusiasm. His lack of dedication to the good of Uncle Walt must have been apparent fairly quickly because, although he was one of the best dancers and all-around performers in the group, he found himself being featured less and less. He also suffered from Disney's attitude against getting experienced professional kids for the show. When Annette became hot, and Walt felt his attitude on the subject had been vindicated, the professional kids like Lonnie and Sharon began to get less attention. By the end of year two he had been cropped from "Roll Call."

He left the Disney organization, like Darlene, somewhat embittered by the experience. They had taken the most valuable seven years of his childhood career, set him loose at an awkward age when parts were difficult to come by, had paid him—and several of the others—less than he would have gotten elsewhere, and had failed to establish him as a star. At fourteen years old, Lonnie's career went into a tailspin. Alienated from his fellow college students by the fact of his age, a loner by inclination anyway, Lonnie began to feel the pain. He went into a James Dean period. He drank too much and drove too fast. He discovered women, among them such Hollywood starlet types as Barbara Parkins, Sherry Jackson, and Brenda Benet.

When he was fifteen, his parents split and Lonnie went to live with his grandparents in Van Nuys. He managed to avoid hurting himself for a couple of years but then some things happened. There were automobile accidents—three of them, in fact.

"The worst one happened in my Volvo," he says. "I was coming through Coldwater Canyon after a party at four in the morning. The other guy was coming from the Valley. I don't know, I suppose I had been drinking a little, but there was a curve and this guy hit me broadside. I still have a few scars from that one."

And, too, there was an attempted suicide.

"I think I just said to myself one day 'I'm twenty years old and nothing I've done matters, really.' I had just gone through a love-affair-rejection kind of thing and I was drinking too much. It was in the bathroom at my grandparents'. I cut my wrists and sat down on the side of the tub to wait for something to happen. Nothing much happened. Finally, a friend came in and said, 'What are you doing' and I said, 'I'm killing myself' and he said, 'You shouldn't ought to do that because it will cause injury to your body.' He ran downstairs to get my grandmother and she came upstairs and I was standing there bleeding on the orange carpet. 'I'm bleeding,' I said and she said, 'Sssssh. Your grandfather's asleep. If he wakes up, he'll kill you.'

"Anyway, my friend drove me down to the doctor who sewed me up . . . none too gently I might add. He kept mumbling about how you people don't know how to do it right and I said, 'Sorry, Doc, I haven't had that much experience at this. I never killed myself before.' Anyway, he finished and I drove over to my girlfriend's house and she cried a little and we balled."

Lonnie credits his unsuccessful suicide attempt with straightening his life out a bit.

"I think it was good in some ways. It got me into therapy which helped enormously and I sort of stopped drinking so much. I don't think the situation will come when I get that desperate again. I think I've learned to control things better and deal with my problems more maturely.

"There was one funny thing about that business, though. It was in one little paper and then suddenly the story disappeared. I've always suspected the Disney people hushed it up."

Lonnie became absorbed with his master's work at UCLA and continued to make some appearances on shows like the "Beverly Hillbillies," "Father Knows Best," and "World of Disney." He did do some traveling and one of the amusing little stories he likes to tell is about running into Tommy Kirk, in Paris to do a film for Disney and loaded with expense money, doing several French bordellos courtesy of Uncle Walt.

In 1968, Lonnie got married to Dahrlene Mitchell, a singer with whom he had lived a couple of years off and on. The marriage lasted less than a year.

I asked Lonnie if I could put a few of his poems in the book and he selected these:

Particular Shadows
Particular Sounds

If I can choose to turn again
If I can choose
If turning chose again
I would not leave volition out of time
I would not try to time the right to choose
Again, it comes to nestle close by breath
the anxious starings sudden sounds impress
the interloper wandering guidelines forth
beyond a reason dribbled past too fast
too fast to hasten fast the present past.

In flight I tread the darkened corridors
of vast and endless space my very own
my very last exchange with light with death
a mute cacophony of leaves on ground
not spun around nor whirled in circles light
but planted firm below the limb bunched green
to lose identity and willful sheen.

Scriptless bottle caps married to macadam
by chance and subtle mercenary ways
as you and I bump up against our walls
sequoias courting proper flower stalls
enchanted chanting rhythms of the night
beguile my once transfixed and somber sight
calling me away from madness
calling me away from sadness
calling me away
calling

If I could choose to turn again
If I could choose
If turning chose again
I would not leave volition out of time
I would not try to time the right to choose

isolation

At a party once
James Joyce and Samuel Beckett
sat and laughed,
Camus and Nietzsche
sat there too
and stared,
Wilde and Rosetti merely cried.
I don't go to parties anymore.

brumal

Lay the hoary frost
          back

to melt,
      anew;

Green orchid dust
        resembles
                your

love

One day I had lunch with Lonnie who had just had dinner the night before with Sharon Baird, who was in town with a touring production of "H. R. Pufnstuf." He seemed shaken by the experience.

"I really got a sense of emptiness out of seeing Sharon again," Lonnie says, pushing his peas around with his fork the way picky eaters always do. "All that you-should-love-your-mother, apple-pie sort of stuff. She didn't use to be that way. Or, at least, I don't think she was. It took me straight back to 1955 and I didn't like it terribly. I don't care what anybody tells you, those were not the good old days."

He stares at the peas with genuine disgust.

"I always thought she should have married Bobby anyway. Poor Bobby. It's hard to dance and be suave in snowshoes, particularly when you're always tripping over your teeth.

"The Mouseketeer business. Wow. I've done a lot of things since that are a lot better and more creative. But the press always seems to fasten on that. They say, 'Oh, you did that.' If I said I was just Hamlet at Stratford and was sensational they'd say, 'Oh, yeah. Great. Now, tell me: What was Annette Funicello really like?'"

5

Darlene— The Unlikely Star

Darlene Gillespie was not what one thought of in the 1950s when one thought of "stars." She was tall and awkward, with freckles and too many teeth. She had a quick mind and a biting cynical tongue. She was not pretty.

But, in the vernacular of Variety, Darlene was a terrific chirp. When she opened her mouth to sing, a kind of magic poured out. She was far and away the most gifted of the Mouseketeers. When she sang "When I Grow Up Someday" or "With a Smile and a Song," director Dick Darley used to pretend he had something in his eye. He wasn't alone.

Some of the other kids found her aloof and overly self-protective but, to this day, nobody denies her enormous talent. And, the fact of the matter is, Darlene was not comfortable on the show. Part of her problem was a simple matter of adjustment. She was fourteen when she came to the Mouse Club, only a month older than Bobby, but considerably older than the rest of the kids. She was confronted by the truly awful prospect, for a gangly teen-ager, of having to go to school with such precociously developed in-

genue types as Annette, Doreen, and Cheryl. This is not even to
mention such sensational young debs as Noreen Corcoran and
Shelley Fabares who frequently worked on the Disney lot and
went to school with the Mouseketeers in the little red trailer at
the studio.

"Puberty didn't hit me until I was in my twenties," Darlene,
once aptly described as a beauty parlor blonde, says with a laugh.
"Oh, I suppose I went through that teen-age crisis where if you
don't have boobs, you think you're not a woman. I was so goddamned untogether that I had to make it on talent, not sex appeal."

Darlene is a remarkably open woman. She is aggressively intelli-
gent and very funny in that cynical sort of put-down-of-self-and-
others way that women are frequently not good at. She is a
fantastic contrast to Annette with her studied innocence and her
protective world in Encino. Darlene has seen life, taken the show
biz lumps, and emerged cynical but real.

Until she resumed singing a couple of years ago, Darlene
worked as a surgical nurse at Valley Presbyterian Hospital.

"It was very rewarding," she said. "We opened people up.
Sometimes they died." It's a fake cynicism, of course, designed to
cover up the fact that one really cares or one wouldn't be there,
among the broken bodies, in the first place.

Darlene was born in Montreal on April 8, 1941, an Aries if you
care about that sort of thing. Her parents, Larry and Dorothy
Gillespie, were—like Lonnie and Doreen's folks—a dance team.
They deserted the theatrically barren rues of Montreal for the
promise of Hollywood when Darlene was three. The Gillespies are
a large family; Darlene has three sisters and two brothers.

"Obviously," Darlene says, with some relish, "they didn't dance
all the time. But, seriously, they were not the typical show business parents. I was very fortunate in that way."

In California, Darlene took dance lessons from Burch Holtzman, the lady whom Bill Walsh and Hal Adelquist had enlisted
to help them find performers for the Mouse Club. That's how she

happened to turn up at one of the early cattle-call auditions for the show.

Although a couple of former Mouseketeers portray Darlene as something of a show biz brat, she actually had less performing experience than most of the others. Her only previous professional job had been cutting a demo record for Jimmy Boyd which he later recorded and which turned out to be a bomb. (Jimmy Boyd was a roommate of Cheryl Holdridge's future husband Lance Reventlow and, you may recall, the singer of the most god-awful song ever recorded, "I Saw Momma Kissing Santa Claus.")

Darlene's audition surprised even her.

"I guess I wasn't so aware of the singing thing," she says. "My mother had a good voice. But I got down there and they asked me if I could sing and I said, 'Sure, I can sing' and I sang."

It quickly became obvious to all those who listened that this unprepossessing package contained something quite special. Darlene was a genuine Hollywood canary.

When the Club premiered on October 3, 1955, the people at Disney studio who believed talent always outs were placing their bets on Darlene. It didn't work out that way.

*   *   *

That Darlene was gifted was obvious. What to do about it was another matter. The Disney organization, long geared to promoting little creatures that moved only on paper, had still not adjusted to the idea of dealing with live people. Bill Walsh featured Darlene in songs and she was eventually cast in the lead of the series "Corky and the White Shadow" with Buddy Ebsen. She sang cornball songs like "Buckwheat Cakes" and "Uncle Dan" and hated the "dumb" white shepherd who was also featured. The series was, she now says, "horrendous" and it failed to generate the kind of mail response that programs featuring Annette did.

"I really don't think Disney was prepared to promote and develop talent in the way some of the other studios like Warners and 20th were," Darlene says. "They played a kind of Russian roulette game. Whoever got the most mail got the most to do . . . even if their mother wrote it."

Which brings us back to the thing about whether Annette's fantastic mail response was legit which we don't need to get into again.

That there was an intense rivalry between Darlene and Annette is undeniable. History has obscured the specifics of the feud but Darlene has a theory.

"I think all those stories about jealousy between Annette and me were largely caused by adults," she says. "Somehow, they tried to make everything competitive, which is a monstrous thing to do to a kid. No wonder kids who get into show business early often have tremendous adjustment problems when they get older. Christ, it's enough to warp your whole value system. Somehow, you are made to think that winning is more important than being a good human being.

"I mean, there's no reason to think Bobby Burgess is a more worthwhile person than anybody else just because he happens to dance on the 'Lawrence Welk Show'—which, incidentally, is not exactly my idea of making it.

"And besides," she says, with a twinkle, "the real reason I never liked Annette is because she always got the new tap shoes. I had to wear the same goddamned shoes until I was eighteen. It nearly crippled me for life."

Darlene pauses a minute to go see what her two-year-old Lisa is doing to her four-month-old David James. "She's been trying to eliminate him from the human race," she says, by way of explanation.

It is impossible, I recall thinking, not to like this woman with her quick wit and her no-bullshit philosophy of life. Why then did so many of the other kids not like her? Was it simply because she was talented? Was it because she was a cynic and in 1955 that was a mistrusted attitude?

"The Disneys really were incredibly cheap," Darlene says, apropos of nothing but it's obviously a subject she wants to get into. "I didn't get anything extra for being featured in 'Corky' and I suspect—but can't prove it—that I've never gotten a fair count on overseas royalties from the records I did for them. Christ, that *Alice in Wonderland* record has sold over a million copies. I see it every once in a while down at Ralph's supermarket. My father checked into it once and somebody at the studio told him 'You're going to need a multimillionaire lawyer if you're going to take on Walt Disney.'

"I don't think they liked my father around the studio because he was kind of a thoughtful, intellectual man. Ever so often, Lee Trevors would come around and say, 'Well, kiddies, Uncle Waltie is giving you a raise.' My father would say, 'Didn't I read in the papers about a new union settlement?' As it always turned out, Uncle Waltie wasn't giving you nothing except what he had to."

"Being older than the others—"

"I wasn't older," Darlene says. "Karen and Cubby were both twenty-four. They were midgets."

"—were you aware of what was going on when people like Hal Adelquist were suddenly not around anymore?" I ask.

"I don't guess I was really," she says. "All I knew was one day Uncle Hal just wasn't there anymore. The same is true of Dick Darley and Sidney Miller. Uncle Dick and Uncle Sid, both of whom were terrific and really knew their business, just vanished into thin air one day. I don't think anybody ever explained to the kids what had happened. Who knows? Maybe they asked the cheap bastards for more money."

Dick Darley, you will recall, directed the show the first year it was on the air. He went on to direct Rosemary Clooney's TV show afterward, still lives in Hollywood, and is one of the more active directors of commercials around. His replacement, Sid Miller, took a more Prussian attitude toward the kids, had them all audition again, and was a tough, but kind, taskmaster.

"I suppose," Darlene says, letting her mind ramble for a moment, "that I saw Walt Disney about five times in my life. He never came around much. He seemed okay but somehow I just got the impression he was a kind of Pontius Pilate who let other people do his dirty work for him. Bill Walsh, on the other hand, was a fantastic man, one of the sharpest, funniest people there. He's extremely talented as I think the things he's done show."

The talk shifts to Jimmie Dodd, about whom Darlene has good feelings.

"Jimmie was a very sweet person," she says. "He was from the old school of show business where the thing to do was to smile a lot and love everybody. But he was really good. Imagine just keeping your wits while you're surrounded by two dozen screaming little bastards. Not to mention the pressure from parents, all of whom think their kid is it. Somehow, he always managed to be fair."

Times got tough for Darlene after the Mouse Club. Oh, there were bit parts on "Dr. Kildare" and "National Velvet," a rather good Alice in Wonderland commercial for Ford, and some nightclub work in Vegas, but, in general, her career went into a decline.

"It was a really bad ego trip for me," she says. "It's a hard thing. Out here the question is not what have you done but what have you done lately. I began to doubt whether I had any talent or not. In a way, I sort of admire someone like Bobby who can manipulate himself into thinking what he's doing is important. If you're going to be in show business, you've got to be prepared to give up so much of yourself. You can't philosophize. To 95 per cent of the people you meet you're 'Let's see it, chicky-baby.' Most of the people you meet in the business are like that."

Darlene made the decision to get out of the business, for good she thought, and went back to school to study nursing. She became an RN, specializing in cardiac surgery at Valley Presbyterian Hospital. Occasionally, a patient would remark, out of the depths of anesthesia, "I know your voice. You're Darlene Gillespie, the Mouseketeer."

About five years ago, she married Philip Gammon, a "nice guy" from Illinois who never watched the "Mickey Mouse Club." Gammon is a successful independent oil and gas operator who owns a string of service stations. With his help, Darlene is about to make a comeback in show business on her own terms.

"Fortunately," Darlene says, "my husband is a wealthy man

and he's formed a record company. It sounds silly to say, I know, but it's true. We've done one record which turned out pretty well, so I'm going to Nashville soon to do some more country and western stuff. . . . I really like country and western. Patsy Cline was my favorite singer. You can learn everything there is to know about singing by listening to that lady's records."

The Gammons' company is called Alva Records and they have great hopes for it, as well as a music publishing firm called Blue Mountain. The hope, of course, is that Darlene will be the star but they also plan to record other singers. In the meantime, Darlene is on an indefinite leave of absence from her nursing job at Valley Presbyterian.

"I'm glad you're getting back into records," I said, "and I'm glad we finally got to talk." Darlene had, I thought, avoided me on a previous trip to Los Angeles.

"So am I, hon," she says. (Darlene says "hon" a lot, the way that nurses and stewardesses and beauty shop girls always do.) "I'll tell you the truth. When you first told me what you were doing, I thought it was pretty silly. I feel better about it now but, this is the truth; if having been a Mouseketeer is the only thing I have to be remembered for, I'd just as soon be forgotten. The Mouseketeers . . . I mean . . . Christ!"

* * *

A few weeks after our talk, Darlene sent me two copies of her new record, some pictures, and a note:

> Dear Jerry:
>
> Sorry to be so late in getting the pictures and record to you but that seems to be the story of my life! But all last week was hell on wheels! Sorry Disney wouldn't help you more but sometimes too much help is a killer! Hope you have a lot of success and that your book on the old mouses gets you into something bigger and better as a writer.

I kept the record around the house two days before I played it. Maybe it was the coy recording name Darlene has taken—Darlene

Valentine—or maybe it was the fact that I really like country and western music, but I was afraid to play it. I grew up in southern West Virginia where country is king and, just to give you an idea of how passionate I am on the subject, Eric Weissberg's clumsy banjo playing makes me want to physically abuse my radio.

I needn't have worried though. One side of the record—"April Is the Month for Loving"—was sensational. Darlene has lost nothing of the magic. It made me feel good; maybe talent eventually wins out, after all.

6

Tommy—
The Nice Guy

Tommy Cole positively radiates inner peace and contentment. His every gesture is a study in rationality and calm. He speaks in the very precise and reassuring monotone of a Lutheran minister. His is a pleasant, sugary voice; the kind you might expect to hear coming from your radio saying something like "It's seventy-four degrees in downtown Los Angeles and, incidentally, the San Andreas fault just swallowed Beverly Hills, but there's nothing to be alarmed about."

Clearly, Tommy is the kind of person who is accustomed to always doing the mature, grown-up thing. One pictures him as a born mediator, a useful go-between, a peacemaker of considerable skill which, anytime two or more kids get together, is a necessary role. In terms of locating people and establishing contacts, he was more than generous with me.

There is something frightening about his insistence upon his own well-being, though. "I'm very happy," he says, at every opportune moment, and his sincerity eludes disbelief.

Like Cubby, Tommy was born practically in Walt Disney's

backyard, in Burbank, on December 20, 1941. His father was a troubleshooter for the Los Angeles *Herald-Examiner* and his mother was "mostly a housewife, although she did do some work as a salesgal."

Tommy is sporting a goatee these days but even that can't conceal the fact that he has retained that pretty-boy look from childhood. There is a curious lack of animation in his movements and his overall bearing is one of studied control.

His major thing on the Mouse Club was singing and he was rather good at it. Next to Darlene, he was the best singer on the show and, because of his pleasant speaking voice, he also did a lot of narration and voice-over work.

Because they were both singers, there was some rivalry between the two and Tommy admits he was never fond of Darlene. By one of those strange tangents that life sometimes takes, the Gammons and the Coles lived for some time across the street from each other in Van Nuys and the two are now good friends.

Tommy's entry into show business was not a smooth one within his family and, in truth, touched off a major family crisis. His grandmother, a staunch Lutheran who felt that television was somehow sinful, was dead set against it. She was finally won over.

Although he had sung at clubs and parades and talent shows, Tommy had one major disadvantage as a Mouseketeer. He had never studied dancing.

"The studio was a little concerned over the fact that I had never danced," Tommy says. "I was given a trial contract with the understanding that I had to be able to keep up with the other kids. I took lessons from Burch Holtzman first, then from Louis de Pron. I never did learn to dance very well but I became an excellent faker . . . and the other kids helped me out a lot, too."

Tommy auditioned for the Club as part of a group. He was the accordion player.

"For some reason," he says, "the casting director took a liking to me and I kept going back for more auditions. Finally, I got the job and I haven't touched an accordion since."

We are talking in my hotel room in Hollywood. Tommy walks

over to the window and looks out. Down there on Hollywood Boulevard below, a woman is pointing toward Marilyn Monroe's footprints in the sidewalk in front of Graumann's Chinese Theatre. Her kid doesn't seem interested.

The way Tommy sees it, the Mouseketeers were all just a bunch of terrific kids and his impressions of the others seem to go out of their way to be charitable.

"Annette was hand-picked by Disney," he says. "That's why she went so far. She was just a plain, flat-chested little girl in the beginning.

"Cubby? He's a real nice kid. And a great musician. He plays drums better than anybody I've ever known. Sharon is just like my little sister. I don't see her as often as I'd like to but she's a real sweetheart. Bobby is, you know, just all teeth but a real nice guy."

He mentions several others but you get the idea.

"Jimmie Dodd . . . well, Jimmie was the most wonderful man I've ever met. I'm sure I'll never meet anyone like him again. He was really unbelievable. They don't make people like him anymore. If you just met him you might think that nobody is that nice or that sweet. But Jim really was that way. He was very religious but he never tried to push. And he had this beautiful red hair. He was just a fantastic man."

After he left the Mouseketeers, Tommy went to Hollywood Professional School and made occasional appearances on "Leave It to Beaver" and "My Three Sons." His mother was a guardian on the latter show.

"I had three recording contracts but then nothing ever came of them," he says, seemingly without remorse. "In my late teens, I decided to do something to stay in the business which I really love. It's a rough life in front of the camera unless you're a star or a character actor. I was just another pretty little all-American boy. I had a fairly good voice but there are a lot of good voices around this town. That's when I first got interested in makeup."

Tommy attended Pasadena College for a couple of years, then began working with a nightclub act called the Andressi Brothers.

When one of the brothers got drafted, Tommy took his place in the act for a time.

"By 1965, my dad's health was not so good and by the next year I was in a really bad way financially. The makeup thing had not really jelled yet. I got a chance to go on tour with Johnny Mathis. I wasn't that crazy about going on the road but I needed the money so I took the job."

One Mathis trip, to the Orient, turned out fortuitously enough. Tommy met his future wife Aileen in Seoul, Korea. Aileen was part of a USO show.

"I only knew her two days there," Tommy says, "but after I got back to the states I wrote to her, we started corresponding, and in 1968 we got married."

Aileen is a stewardess for United Airlines. She started back to work a couple of years ago.

"She wanted to work," Tommy says, "and I think it's good, although I don't see her as much as I might like right now. I put her through hairdresser school because I thought it would be nice for us to be in sort of the same field. That petered out."

Tommy seems animated for the first time in the conversation. "That's a rough business," he says. "You get all those bitchy women. A male hairdresser has an advantage in that he can simply tell them to shove it and get by with it. Another woman can't do that. I can be rougher and stronger in my work."

By the time Tommy came back from the Johnny Mathis tour, he had had it, he says, with the suitcase life. The idea of becoming a makeup man, which had been in the back of his mind for several years, came to the fore.

"I went down to ABC and gave them a lot of bullshit. Oh, I knew basic makeup but it takes time to get confidence in your work. Half of the business is personality, being able to get along with people. Finally, by simply being persistent, a job opened up and I got it. I really love my job now. I'm very happy in my work."

Now I happen to believe that, but I did ask an acquaintance of Tommy's about his professed contentment and got "Balls. All he ever wanted to be was Bing Crosby. He just didn't have the talent."

Tommy is now a staff makeup artist at KNBC in Burbank, working mainly on daytime soap operas.

"They're great shows," he says, a hint of irony creeping across his imperturbable face. "Everybody's sleeping with everybody else. But . . . it keeps the housewives happy."

Tommy says he doesn't miss being in front of the camera for a moment. The Mouseketeer experience was obviously one of the most important of his life and, he, more than any of the others, sort of keeps track of what has happened to kids who appeared on the show. As I said, it was he who was most helpful to me in locating many of them.

"It was a great part of my life," he says. "We all got along. There weren't that many petty jealousies. Oh, there were a few stage mothers, but kids who were problems were dropped pretty quick.

"I just wouldn't want to go back to performing . . . with all the uncertainty that that involves. I guess I'm just very settled. I don't have to go to an analyst. I don't hit the wall very often. I guess I'm very fortunate. I look around me and I see other people whose lives are screwed up and I just thank my lucky stars."

Annette won viewers' hearts easily just by being herself. (Wide World)

Annette with one of her millions of admirers. (UPI)

Annette displays the smile that made "puppy love" a real experience for thousands of teen-age boys in the 1950s. (UPI)

Did they or didn't they? Annette and Frankie Avalon kept moviegoers guessing in a series of Beach pictures. (UPI)

Annette and family. Gina, ten, newcomer Jason, and Jack, Jr., six. (Wide World)

It broke Charlie Brown's heart but on January 9, 1965, Annette married her agent, Jack Gilardi. (Wide World)

7

Cheryl

Cheryl Holdridge Reventlow was walking down an Aspen street not long ago when she was stopped by a most excited man in his early thirties. "Don't I know you?" he said. Cheryl, who was rather flattered, said it was quite possible since—as a matter of fact—she used to appear on television. "Ah, yes," the man said, after a moment of intense reflection. "I know. You were Wally's girlfriend on 'Leave It to Beaver'!" But, of course.

"Of all the dumb things to be remembered for," Cheryl says, tossing those lovely blond curls that charmed many a studio executive in the mid-fifties. "Isn't that just . . . dynamite?" The general's daughter from Sherman Oaks who grew up to be one of the world's younger, prettier, and wealthier widows chuckles at the thought.

Cheryl Holdridge's story is the kind of thing of which Hollywood myth is made. She is the beautiful young starlet who met, fell in love with, and married the handsome and rich playboy.

Not since Shirley Temple first took the matrimonial plunge has there been the kind of excitement that filled the air inside Westwood Community Methodist Church on November 8, 1963, when Lance Reventlow, son of Woolworth heiress Barbara Hutton and Count Court Haugwitz Hardeberg Reventlow, second of Barbara's seven husbands, exchanged vows with Cheryl, the darling little ex-Mouseketeer.

The engagement had been announced eleven months before, but Lance had had to have time to work out a rather sticky divorce with his first wife, Jill St. John. Cheryl told reporters that the romance had really gotten serious when Ms. St. John and Reventlow had ironed out their property settlement differences late in 1963. "And," she added, "I stopped dating Elvis."

When a reporter brought up Reventlow's reputation as an international playboy, Cheryl bristled. "That's unfair. He's sweet and honest and just wonderful."

One thing for sure, there were few catches in the world quite like Lance Reventlow. He was handsome and he was rich, called at birth "the world's richest baby." As Barbara Hutton's only child, he stood to inherit the Woolworth fortune.

He was also daring. Lance dropped out of college to learn motorcar racing. Shortly after his twenty-first birthday—at which time he came into $25 million—Reventlow hired fourteen car experts and set up shop in L.A. to create an American sports car that could outrace the great Europeans. The result was the Scarab, named after an Egyptian good-luck charm. In 1958, Reventlow and two teammates, driving the Scarabs, consistently beat the Ferraris and Maseratis in international competition.

Mouseketeer Cheryl was only fourteen that year, doing her bit on the Mouse Club, which was mostly dancing and skits, and acquiring the reputation for being the biggest tomboy on her block in Sherman Oaks.

Late in 1958, on December 5, Reventlow scored his first important victory in Nassau when he drove a Chevrolet-powered Scarab to an easy win in the 112.5-mile Governor's Cup race, marking the first time since 1924 that an American car and driver had won an international road race.

Reventlow's success on the race courses of the world had a bad effect on his marriage, though. When Jill St. John walked out in 1963, she blamed the split on Lance's passion for sports cars.

Cheryl first met Lance at a party and took an immediate liking

to him. He was forceful. He knew what he liked. He disapproved
of the music being played and drove home to get some John Lee
Hooker and Jimmy Reed records.

"Lance loved to cook for people," Cheryl says. "We went out
several times and he would invite me up to his house for dinner.
Then, I don't know, he went off racing and we sort of lost touch
for a while."

Cheryl was a Hollywood ingenue by this time, doing the things
that starlets do to keep their names before the public. She was
dating Elvis Presley with some regularity and insists that it was
not simply a publicity ploy. Of course, it appears in retrospect
that Elvis was simply waiting for his true love—now his ex-wife—
to grow up (literally), and thus his forays into the wild, strawberry-blond world of Hollywood starlets would have to be judged
less than serious. Cheryl remembers him fondly, though.

"Elvis is a dynamite man," she says. "He's an adult and one of
the nicest and kindest people in the world. He liked to just sit
around and talk."

As for Cheryl, she was seeing on a more serious level a young
British actor named Michael Anderson to whom she became
"semiengaged." In December of 1963, Anderson went back to
England for a visit, presumably to tell his parents of his impend-
ing happy event. He shoulda stood in town.

"A funny thing happened," says Cheryl, in a classic case of un-
derstatement. "I went to a party one night and Lance was there. I
hadn't seen him for a long time. We started rapping and, I don't
know, about three weeks later we decided to get engaged."

For Cheryl, the Sherman Oaks tomboy, those Saturdays helping
the neighborhood boys adjust the timer on their carburetors was
to pay big dividends.

"One day Lance let me drive one of his Scarabs and we took off
over the hill toward Benedict Canyon. I was going pretty fast and
there was a curve up ahead. I had no choice but to downshift. I
made it all the way down to first without scraping a gear. I think
that's when he knew he had made the right choice."

What could be more . . . perfect, more California?

Recognizing that a Hollywood starlet is the devil's playground and that southern California has lots of handsome, rich dudes, Lance showered his new treasure with gifts. A mink coat here. A sports car there. A side order of diamonds.

He needn't have worried. Cheryl wasn't about to break loose. After Sharon's wedding to Lee Thomas, Cheryl and a few of the ex-Mouseketeers went to the Luau, a Hollywood restaurant for drinks. When the maître d' expressed regrets over not having a table, Cheryl informed him that she was Mrs. Lance Reventlow—which she wasn't at the time—and that if he knew what was good for him, he'd damn well find one. He found one.

One of Lance's gifts, a foreign sports car, turned out to be something of a problem.

"It was an Iso Rivolta which, as a matter of fact, is a pretty good description of the thing," she says. "It was always breaking down."

The car's most celebrated breakdown came on the day Lance and Cheryl went for their marriage license. They were to arrive separately but the Iso stalled, so Cheryl made a frantic call. Lance dashed off in his Corvette to pick her up and they raced to the county clerk's office in Santa Monica, getting there shortly after the 4:30 P.M. closing time. Cheryl, smashing in a pair of purple capris, hopped out of the car and sprinted into the building, only to return a few moments later throwing her hands up in a gesture of despair. Reventlow, who was somewhat publicity shy, spotted several newsmen and he and Cheryl raced off. They got their license the next morning in Glendale.

The wedding itself went smoother. About six hundred guests, heavily laden with show biz types, jammed inside Westwood Methodist for the thirty-minute ceremony.

Oh, there were a couple of hitches. The bridegroom's mother, then Princess Champacak, did not attend but remained in Paris on the advice of her doctors. She didn't forget a wedding gift, however. Ms. Hutton picked up the tab on a five-bedroom, six-bath country home in Benedict Canyon. It was a heavy tab, with rumors running around $250,000.

The only "relative" of Lance to attend was Cary Grant. Grant, a former husband of Ms. Hutton and thus Lance's ex-stepfather, came with a gorgeous young actress named Dyan Cannon.

The other hitch was Cheryl's parents who were in the middle of a major spat. Bill Mellinthen, a friend of the family, gave the bride away in the absence of retired Brigadier General Herbert C. Holdridge, who apparently was not invited. The first newspaper accounts of the wedding had said he wouldn't be there because of illness. However, in a letter to UPI dated two days before the ceremony, General Holdridge said he wasn't coming because "Cheryl and her mother don't want me there."

In defense of the ladies, the good general had been subject to—well, erratic behavior in recent years. He had run for President in 1952 as a candidate of the American Rally Party and, although not a teetotaler, had represented the Prohibition Party in 1956. He wrote odd letters to people.

Strangely, the general was more left than right in his thinking. Someone recently gave me a membership card from the American Rally Party which was headquartered at 11806 Woodward Avenue in Detroit. The "aims" of the party are listed on the back:

1. For permanent peace now on all fronts
2. For expanding abundance for all, through a non-profit economy.
3. For full constitutional, political, and economic democracy.
4. For fulfillment of purposes through constitutional, non-violent means.
5. For General Herbert C. Holdridge for President of the United States.

"I guess he's still alive," Cheryl told me. "We haven't had much communication in recent years. I'm really sorry about what has happened to him. I loved him very much. I still do."

In any event, General Holdridge was not there.

Cheryl, nineteen, was absolutely radiant. You could hear the gasps as she walked down the aisle. Guests were so enthralled by the storybook quality of the thing that they forgot to sit down, so everyone stood throughout the entire ceremony.

The supporting cast was magnificent, also. Eight pretty young bridesmaids in Beauty Rose full-length gowns and maid of honor Doreen Tracey, in shocking pink, not to mention the brunette wig Cheryl had insisted she wear so as not to clash.

The ushers, in full rig, were entertainers Jimmy Boyd and Ronnie Burns, Tom Skouras, son of Twentieth Century Fox exec Spiros Skouras, ex-ski champions Yves Latreille and Jack Reddish, and Charles Rosher, Gary Wooten, and Dan Busby.

The best man was movie producer Bruce Kessler, a friend of Lance since childhood. Julie Holdridge, beaming in a full-length blue taffeta gown, followed the script and shed a few tears.

Outside, on the church patio, the happy couple formed a receiving line to greet well-wishers and to oblige photographers who kept asking them to kiss "just once more." "I think you guys are on my side," Lance said, with a sheepish grin.

Finally, the newlyweds slipped into a waiting Cadillac and left to host a champagne reception for three hundred at Reventlow's home.

It was one of those almost perfect days, when the joy of being young and beautiful and rich and loved seemed enough to chase the uglies away forever.

The next day Lance and Cheryl left for Hawaii for a month-long honeymoon. It was one of life's terrible little ironies that as the happy couple descended from the plane at the Honolulu airport, Jimmie Dodd was less than twenty-four hours from death in a nearby hospital. It was a terrible reminder that for every opening act there is a final curtain.

Maybe, just maybe, it was an omen.

*   *   *

There is a touch of mystery to Cheryl's beginnings. Born in New Orleans on June 20, 1944, Julie Holdridge brought her to Sherman Oaks when she married General Holdridge. Few, if any, of the other Mouseketeers knew that Cheryl was an adopted child.

Cheryl was an incredibly pretty little girl with a sweet disposition. Her mother was certain that she had another Shirley Temple on her hands. Naturally, Cheryl took ballet lessons (from Joyce Cole in North Hollywood) and she was a member of a Bluebird troop whose particular thing was dancing. She turned pro at age nine, landing one of the child leads, Clara, in the New York City Ballet's version of *The Nutcracker Suite* which was an annual affair at the Greek Theatre in Los Angeles.

"It was just a dynamite experience for a nine-year-old," Cheryl says. "I loved doing it and, as a matter of fact, I did it the next year too."

By age ten, Cheryl had acquired some of the trappings of show biz, most notably an agent, and she was doing TV commercials ("Good morning, Miss Dove," "Carousel").

"I didn't go out for the Mouseketeers the first year," Cheryl says, "although I did try out for a part in 'The Hardy Boys.' My agent didn't really want me to go over to Disney because she thought we could make more money elsewhere.

"Anyway, I had this girlfriend, see, and she told me she was going to be a Mouseketeer. Well, that did it. I wasn't going to have some friend of mine being a Mouseketeer and not me, so, unbeknownst to my mother and my agent, I rang up Lee Trevors at Disney and arranged to come over for an interview.

"It really blew my mind. There was a big hall and hundreds of kids and Bill Walsh and Mr. Disney were there. It was a terrifying experience. I sang 'Davy Crockett' . . . badly, and I forgot my dance. And, afterward, I was called up to the table to talk and I couldn't think of anything to say.

"I just knew I had blown it and I guess my mother did too because I remember she was very sweet to me in the car on the way home. A few days later, I got a call to report to the studio. And, more than that, out of the new kids only Jay Jay Solari and I were put into Roll Call."

Cheryl quickly became friends with Doreen who, being older and wiser, took her under her wing. Doreen's precocious physical development was a bit intimidating, however.

"It wasn't too much fun going to the beach with Doreen," she says. "She's really stacked. I started to get an inferiority complex about it. Here comes Doreen bopping along in a bikini and me trailing along all wrapped up in a blanket. I could barely fill my top up."

As a matter of fact, the first time Cheryl went water skiing she picked it up right away and was sailing along when she happened to look down and discovered that she had lost the top half of her swimsuit.

"In a way," she says, "I think that was a major part of Darlene's trouble on the show. She was enormously talented but very bitter. She was an ugly duckling with a lot of talent who just wanted to be beautiful. And she was surrounded by girls who were."

After the MMC, Cheryl emerged as a full-blown ingenue on "The Donna Reed Show," "Ozzie and Harriet," "Bachelor Father," "My Three Sons," "Leave It to Beaver," "Dobie Gillis," and "Dennis the Menace." She was cast in the lead role of Betty in a series based on the "Archie" comic books but it never got past the pilot.

"I enjoyed being the starlet," she says. "It's wonderful to have people make a fuss over you, although I don't care for it as much now. True, nobody ever asked you how you felt about the State of the Union or anything like that. But, it was a lot of fun."

* * *

It's hard to say exactly when things started to go bad for Lance and Cheryl. It wasn't even that they were bad. He just began to spend more of his time in Aspen and she stayed mainly in L.A. They talked every day by phone, often for hours. The phone bills were staggering.

"The only thing legal about our relationship, I guess, was our marriage," Cheryl says. "He was my very best friend. We had our own kind of relationship which a lot of people might not understand. But he really was my dearest and closest friend. He didn't want to be in L.A. and I didn't want to be in Colorado, that's all. I loved him so very much. I really did."

* * *

"One of my regrets in life," Cheryl says, "is that Lance never met Jimmie. We went over to the hospital to see him the day we arrived in Honolulu for our honeymoon. He was asleep when we got there. I wanted very much for him to meet Lance. We left him a note.

"I don't know if he saw it or not. Ruth was very sweet. She told me he woke up during the night and saw the note. I hope he did. She's a very nice woman and she may just have been being kind. The next morning he was dead."

* * *

After the "Mickey Mouse Club" ended, Cheryl went back to Van Nuys high school and continued to work in television. She graduated at sixteen and went on the Mouseketeer tour to Australia led by Jimmie and Ruth Dodd.

For three mad, romantic weeks, she had a crush on a kid named Lucky Starr, the biggest Australian rock singer of the period.

"It was a wild, funny three weeks," she says. "People chasing us down the street and all that. The Australians were crazy about the Mouseketeers."

Back home, she grew up as the perfect girl next door. She was athletic and tomboy. She could slide into second and she could throw curve and she tended to say things like: "It was a break-up. You know, a gas, a ball, a blast." She was a nice kid.

"I think I was extremely lucky with parents," she says. "They insisted that I go to public school. They never let me get spoiled and they were firm, but affectionate. I guess that kind of stuff is considered namby-pamby now."

* * *

"So you were born with brown eyes. I was born with money. It just makes life more convenient," Lance Reventlow often told friends.

After he married Cheryl, it appeared that Lance had really, finally, settled down. He became less active in racing and turned his attention to the more sedate pursuits of polo and skiing.

On the morning of July 24, 1972, he took off with three friends —Clifford Hooker, Robert Wulf, and Barbara Baker—to survey a tract of land he wanted to buy near Aspen.

The plane, a single-engine Cessna 206, slammed into a wooded mountainside eight miles from the nearest road. There had been a heavy thunderstorm. The plane never should have gone up.

A few hours later, rescue workers reached the site and confirmed that Lance and his companions were dead. A charmed life had come to its end.

Although they were not officially living together at the time, Lance left the bulk of his fortune—estimated by *Newsweek* at $100 million—to Cheryl. Other magazines used the figure $50 million. Cheryl says she honestly doesn't know.

"Lance left me enough money so I'll never have to work," she says. "I'll never have to need things from people. I'm not in the category of a Doris Duke or anything like that. . . . Look, if I said to you I have over a million, would that do it?"

* * *

Cheryl divides her time these days between Aspen and Los Angeles. She is active in Democratic politics and is involved with the Southern California division of the American Civil Liberties Union. Politically, she's a chip off the old Holdridge block.

Cheryl is an elusive, moody person and there are a lot of things about her which are difficult to explain, or even to know. Why, for example, does she spend so much time now in Aspen, the place Lance loved most in the world, when his being there was one of the things that separated them while they were married? Why does she sometimes in the middle of a phone conversation begin talking about Lance in the present and future tenses ("Lance says, Lance is, Lance will be . . .") as if he'd only stepped out for a short run down the mountain?

Is it real or is it theater? Love? Guilt? What? I think about it a lot.

An old high school girlfriend stays with Cheryl in Aspen. She spends a lot of time reading and skiing and tending her plants. Sometimes there are visitors. Last summer, she met Willy Brandt.

"I guess I don't mind being alone," Cheryl says. "I suppose I'd remarry if Mr. Right came along but marriage is really hard work and I don't think you should do it unless you're prepared to make the investment. I'd like to have kids sometime and I guess I'm old-fashioned but I'd like to be married for that.

"I've had a lot of fun and a lot of sadness in my life already but, for the most part, I think I've lucked out. Some people live charmed and lucky lives and I think I'm one of those people."

8

Bobby

Bobby Burgess has this little joke he likes to play on fans who come up to talk with him after Lawrence Welk performances around the country. When they ask about his wife, Kristie, daughter of Welk's ace accordion player and heir apparent Myron Floren, Bobby says "She's fine. Wantta see a picture?" He whips out an awful photo of an unfortunate young lady whose face appears to have had a tragic confrontation with a truck. It is definitely not Kristie, who is blond and quite pretty. Bobby thinks the gag is amusing. Most often, the folks he plays it on think so too.

"I got caught on that one myself the other day," Bobby says, the inevitable grin spreading across his good-looking, Andy Hardy face. The grin has become his show business trademark. Jimmy Durante had his nose. Jack Benny had his fiddle. Bobby has this ear-to-ear smile which is unmistakable. "We were down in Texas. I'm sitting there in a coffee shop having breakfast with my father-in-law and this guy comes in and says 'Hey, you're on the Lawrence Welk Show and you were Mouseketeer Bobby.' We got to talking and he says, after a while, 'Say, you want to see a picture of my wife?' and like a dummy I say sure. Well, you wouldn't believe this picture."

Bobby grins again. It is an automatic reflex with him, this wide-

eyed grin, as if some cynical charm teacher had frozen his face
into a permanent gee whizz. A vague thought crosses my mind
that the cartoonist who drew the Bucky Beaver Ipana commercials—which were shown a lot on the "Mickey Mouse Club"—just
might have gotten his inspiration from hanging around the
Mouseketeer set watching Bobby.

With the possible exception of his ex-Mouseketeer dancing
partner Sharon Baird, Bobby is the most openly enthusiastic of
the kids who appeared on the show. He is, in want-ad parlance, a
"self-starter." He was the first of the former Mouseketeers to respond to my letter outlining plans for this book.

Bobby writes in an elaborate, childish, nutty hand, marked by
lots of waves and curls. Several ex-Mice use this style. It was perfected by Bobby and Tommy Cole during long boring summer af-
ternoons at Disneyland signing autographs, and it is sort of the
"official Mouseketeer style." As for content, Bobby's letters
exude the kind of wholesome self-centeredness that is not uncom-
mon in actors and children:

> Dear Mr. Bowles,
>
> You're right! "The Mickey Mouse Club" was a very popular
> show in the Fifties. And I was proud to be part of it. What a
> good time we had, and many great memories.
>
> I'd be happy to talk to you about the Mouse Days and an-
> swer any questions you might have.
>
> Lawrence Welk keeps me busy touring when I'm not making
> the television show. I'll be gone March 1st til the 12th of
> March and then March 24th til April 1st. I hope we can get
> together.
>
> Sincerely,
> Bobby Burgess
>
> P.S.   Watch for my partner and I on Johnny Carson Feb.
> 20th.

Enclosed with Bobby's letter was an autographed picture. He never forgets to enclose an autographed picture.

Bobby meets me in my hotel in Los Angeles and we go up to the rooftop restaurant to chat and have a drink. The waitress, a phenomenal brunette in a short, frilly black costume, flashes Bobby a smile of recognition. Even today, in the slumbertime of its soul, Hollywood still is filled with incredible women—would-be starlets from Omaha and Topeka, homecoming queens, handsome creatures with long flouncy manes and long, long legs, all working as waitresses and car hops and beauty shop attendants, all waiting for the proverbial big break. Lana Turner lives.

"Let me get rid of this," Bobby says, undoing a bow tie. He is dressed in the "Great Gatsby" look which is of the moment but which suits him perfectly. He settles back and orders a sweet rum collins.

"Do you believe in astrology," he says. "I'm really not into this star business but I'm a Taurus and I really do seem to have those characteristics. I like security. I like the idea of having something steady. People come up to me all the time and say why don't you leave Welk and step into something better, more exciting. Go do something bigger and better. But I like the idea of a steady income and steady recognition."

Bobby was the tallest and oldest boy among the Mouseketeers so, naturally, he danced mainly with Sharon who was the shortest. Maybe it was just the grin but several of the kids thought he was a goody-goody. Somehow he always seemed to avoid all the smoking, cursing, and fooling around—things that occupied many of the others. He was steady, reliable, talented, enthusiastic, co-operative and well-behaved. Of all the Mouseketeers, he's the only one who's never been out of work.

"Dick Darley loaned me some pictures for a couple of days," I say, handing Bobby a scrapbook. He takes it eagerly.

"Wow," he says, flipping through the pages. "These are just great.

"This one," he says, pointing to a picture of himself and Sharon, "was called 'Cookin' with Minnie Mouse.' Wow. I haven't seen this stuff in years." He turns the page. "This was the other team, the ones who weren't on Roll Call. They did the Guest Stars and the Circus days. We were the Talent Round-Up and the Fun With Music days and occasionally the Anything Can Happen."

"You were on the red team," I say, mainly to show I'd done some research. Just for the sake of historical accuracy, it might be noted here that the major Mouseketeer part of the MMC was the second segment which changed every day: Monday was "Fun With Music Day," Tuesday was "Guest Star Day," Wednesday was "Anything Can Happen Day," Thursday was "Circus Day," and Friday was "Talent Round-Up Day."

Our waitress, Miss Morris Hills High School of 1966, brings a new round, favoring Bobby with another of those I-know-who-you-are smiles. Bobby smiles back, warmly.

"How long have you been dancing?"

"Since I was five years old," he says. "Always with a partner. I danced with a girl named Judy Lewis until I was eight. I danced with a girl named Barbara after the show and, of course, Sharon on the show. Now, it's Bobby and Cissie. I can't seem to get out of that partners rut.

"Anyway, what I was going to say is, I did about seventy-five talent shows between eight and twelve. I remember thinking when I got called to the Mouse Club: 'Gee, this is great. I finally have a steady job.' How do the other kids feel about their experiences on the show?"

"So far," I say, "it splits right down the middle between those who are positive about it and those who are negative."

"I really enjoyed the show," Bobby says. "I'm an ultrapositive. I can tell you who the negatives might be. Lonnie . . . Doreen . . . maybe, Darlene.

"Darlene had an awful lot of talent. She was the one we all thought would go on to become a star. But, from what we could figure out, the studio pushed Annette, and Darlene and her folks became kind of bitter. Darlene was a real good singer and dancer and comedienne but she wasn't a real good actress like Annette.

Annette was warm and natural when she acted. Oh, Darlene had 'Corky and the White Shadow' and it was good but I always thought maybe she didn't have that natural thing as an actress. She could mess around and be really funny, though."

Bobby flips through a few more pages in the photo album.

"This is Bronson Scott," he says, pointing to a very pretty little blond girl. "I dated her a few times. She was such a pretty little girl, just real cute. Then she became such a . . . she misbehaved so much that they had to let her go. The last time I heard she was living with her mother in El Monte. Jeez, she was cute though."

"I wonder," I say, "how you arrived at the idea of who is positive and who is negative about the show. You haven't seen the people much since, so that must have been your impression of them at the time."

Bobby studies the top of his glass for a moment.

"It was their outlook . . . even then. Like things haven't gone the way they probably thought they might for them in show business. It's been pretty hard for most of them I know, because so many times with kid stars they grow up and, I don't know, maybe they don't get the breaks or maybe they haven't prepared themselves enough for what might come up. Show business is a mighty competitive business and there are a lot of disappointments."

Bobby leans forward as if about to share a secret.

"I think a lot of us felt, me included, that since we had been on the Mouse Club we could just go out and say, hey, I was a Mouseketeer. Give me a job. It just didn't work out that way. Like today, for example, I just went out for a commercial. Here I've been on the Welk Show every week for twelve years and on the Mouse Club for four years before that and here I am competing against forty other people including Joe Smith who's done maybe nothing. It's a weird business."

Bobby shakes his head in disbelief.

"Maybe that's why some of the kids from the show are bitter today," he says. He turns another page.

"This is Hal Adelquist. . . . I was talking to Doodles Weaver.

Do you know who he is? He used to do voices and be with Spike
Jones. Anyway, I asked him whatever happened to Uncle Hal?
We were going to make a movie called *The Rainbow Road to Oz*
right after all the Mouseketeers got let go. It got on to the TV
shows but never got released as a movie and Doodles was going to
do my voice. Anyway, I went to the Golden Globes the other day
and saw Doodles and I asked him whatever happened to Hal
Adelquist. He used to not only be a producer but he'd throw parties for us and everything. Apparently Hal turned into a real wino,
an alcoholic, which is a real shame."

Hal Adelquist is a name that comes up frequently in talking to
people about the "Mickey Mouse Club." A lot of folks were really
fond of him. As pieced together from various sources, the mystery
of Hal Adelquist goes like this:

Disney put an increasing amount of heat on Adelquist over the
"Mickey Mouse Club" as the months moved on. Several present
and former studio executives attribute the Disney attack to sheer
jealousy over the phenomenal success of the show. In any event,
by the end of year two Adelquist was no longer involved in
the day-to-day production of the Club. Those who know him say
he began to drink more heavily. For a while, he headed the Disney Talent Round-Up, a kind of organized search and seizure of
the nation's department stores for talented young banjo players.
For a producer of Adelquist's talents it was the death knell. "One
day," Darlene Gillespie says, "Uncle Hal just wasn't there
anymore."

Several months after my conversation with Bobby I called Jack
Lavin, who headed casting at the Disney studio for many years, to
ask if he knew where Adelquist was today. He said the last he
heard, Adelquist was in a hospital. He promised to ask him to call
me if he saw him. No one ever did.

"I don't think Hal was badly treated," Lavin said. "After all,
he got to work directly with Mr. Walt Disney. You can't do any
better than that."

"My being on the show was quite a sacrifice for my mother,"
Bobby says. "She had to spend an hour on the freeway each day to

take me to the studio and to sit there all day waiting for me to finish shooting. It was really quite a sacrifice for her."

Bobby commuted daily from his home in Long Beach, about fifty miles south of Los Angeles. He was born there on May 19, 1941. His father was a meatcutter, his mother a housewife.

He first came to the Disney studio to audition for a role in "Spin & Marty," the serial. The role he wanted had already gone to Tim Considine but Jack Lavin suggested that he audition for the Mouse Club. He did, was called back five times, then hired. Lavin became kind of a protector and once in Chicago when an overly excited fan grabbed Bobby's Mouse ears, it was he who chased her down and retrieved them.

"The thing that made Bobby stand out," one Disney executive recalls, "was his dancing. All the other kids did tap routines. He did a jazz number . . . barefoot . . . to 'Rock Around the Clock.' He was really quite good, even then."

It was Bobby's dancing that made him stand out as a Mouseketeer. More properly, perhaps, it was the fact that he danced with Sharon, a phenomenal hoofer, that made him stand out. They both liked to dance fast and do a lot of acrobatics and were perfectly suited as a team. Bobby's dancing has always been characterized by more athleticism than grace—more Muhammad Ali than Fred Astaire. Bobby does his own choreography for the Welk Show and, in fact, some of the numbers he performs today are simply variations on routines learned as a Mouseketeer.

"You haven't asked me about Walt Disney," Bobby says. "Usually, that's the first thing people ask me. . . . I knew him, of course. He came around and was friendly. But, you know, I don't think anybody really knew him. Maybe some of the adults did. I'm not sure."

Bobby went almost straight from the Mouse Club to the Welk Show although he did manage to finish all but nine units on a B.S. in theater arts at Long Beach State. He joined the Sigma Chi fraternity and is rather proud of the fact that wherever he performs he can usually count on a good turnout from the brothers.

He is also, for what it's worth, friendly with Pat Nugent and danced at his wedding to Luci Bird Johnson.

His clean-cut, boyish image is a strange blend of show biz and junior executive. Bobby is, in fact, something of an entrepreneur who invests his money prudently. He now owns three apartment houses in Long Beach and another in Studio City.

"I used some of the Mickey Mouse money and, of course, some money from Welk to invest in buildings," he says. "I guess it's just that Taurus thing again. I like security. Like, sometimes I say to myself I should quit working and go back and get my degree. But then, I say, that's just crazy."

Outside it has grown dark. Off to the west, the lights of Century City, once the greatest movie lot in the world and now a collection of neocorporate, *nouveau* nothing buildings, wink half-heartedly. Bobby talks on. He loves the past, it is clear. He holds it, embellishes it, caresses it. There was the sweater that Cubby's mother made for him, the trip to Australia, the time Bonnie Kern spat on him when he lifted her overhead during a dance number, the fact that Cheryl really liked him at one point, which is only important because she is now so rich. It is a curious thing, how people make use of the past. For some, 1955 is a slow and torturous cruise to Antarctica; for Bobby, it's a brisk walk to the corner.

"On this thing we were talking about before," Bobby says, turning oddly serious. "I suppose if I hadn't been successful in the business I might be bitter too.

"I mean, it is true that Lawrence Welk is kind of like an adult 'Mickey Mouse Club.' We still have to stand around, yeah, and cheer. Lawrence is a Pisces and he changes his mind a lot. If you want him to do something, you've got to make him think it was his idea first and then, wow, he's all for you. He pays about the same as Disney too . . . very little . . . very much scale."

The waitress brings a new round but this time Bobby doesn't return the smile.

"The best thing about the Welk Show is when we all stand around and say, 'Yeah, Arthur. Atta boy, Arthur.' How about that?" he says. "Sometimes I think, 'Gee, I've been doing this since I was thirteen years old.'"

The look of seriousness lingers for a long moment. An instant of self-doubt, perhaps, or maybe nothing at all. Then, just as suddenly, his face brightens again.

"Hey," he says, the grin back in place. "I almost forgot. I'm going to be on 'Dinah Shore' on the seventeenth. Don't forget to watch."

9

Mickey

Since his appearance in the first cartoon talkie—*Steamboat Willie* in 1928—Mickey Mouse has become the best-known, most-loved star in the history of motion pictures. It seems unlikely at this point in history that there is anybody anywhere who has not seen at least one of his cartoons. In addition, he is almost certainly the most familiar marketing symbol in the world. Mr. Mouse is now in semiretirement and living in Beverly Hills. He consented to a brief interview for this book.

BOWLES: What, in your opinion, are the qualities that have made you the single, best-known personality of the twentieth century?
MOUSE: I don't know. . . . I mean, who really knows in this crazy business? In terms of image, I suppose it's that old saw about the meek shall inherit the earth. Everybody can identify with the shy, quiet little fellow who in the end gets the fat cats. Mr. Charlie Chaplin, for example, was pretty much doing the same thing with his Tramp character. As for my own career, I think it was helped most by my early decision to get into product identification. That gave me some security when the animation films went out.
BOWLES: There is some mystery about how you got into show business. Can you clear that up?

MOUSE: Certainly. I know this is going to sound like the old Schwab drugstore number but I met Mr. Walt Disney on a train from New York to Los Angeles in the spring of 1927. As you may know, Mr. Disney badly needed a star image at the time. He had made over a hundred short features by then and none of them had really caught on. He asked me if I'd like to be in pictures. It's as simple as that. We made two silents—*Plane Crazy* and *Gallopin' Gaucho*—and then we did the first talkie cartoon which, as everybody knows, was *Steamboat Willie* in 1928, and my career, and Mr. Disney's, was launched.

BOWLES: Is Mick—

MOUSE: I should mention here, I suppose, to give credit where credit is due that it was a gentleman named Ub Iwerks who most gave form to my image. Mr. Disney conceived the image; Mr. Iwerks executed it.

BOWLES: Is Mickey Mouse your real name?

MOUSE: Come now, that kind of thing is in the studio bio. I thought this was going to be a serious interview. But since you asked, my real name was Mortimer Mouse. It was Mrs. Disney, I believe, who suggested that Mickey had a more common touch.

BOWLES: How did you meet Donald Duck, Minnie, Goofy, Pluto, and the rest of the Disney gang?

MOUSE: Well, Minnie and I were cast together from the first picture on. Pluto had bit parts in *The Chain Gang* and *The Picnic* around 1930, but he didn't start getting the really good supporting parts until a little later. Goofy was discovered as an extra in *Mickey's Revue* in 1932. Donald came in, I think it was around 1934. Yes, that's it. He had one line in *The Wise Little Hen*.

BOWLES: There were rumors that you and he didn't really get on that well.

MOUSE: The press has a tendency to exaggerate these things. Donald was a star in his own right and he really was a little temperamental. He wanted the part I got in *Fantasia* very badly and was disappointed when Mr. Disney gave it to me. We still work together on TV once in a while and there's no bad blood between us really.

The old and the new Lonnie Burr. (Photo by Bob Breakstone—Courtesy Lonnie Burr)

Cheryl Holdridge does the Hollywood starlet bit in this 1962 photograph. (Wide World)

Cheryl and Lance oblige photographers with a few kisses after the ceremony on November 8, 1964. (Wide World)

Cheryl's adopted father, General Herbert C. Holdridge, ran for President a couple of times and was a founder of the American Rally Party. (UPI)

Cheryl's wedding to Lance Reventlow attracted a lot of big stars like Cary Grant and Dyan Cannon. Grant was once married to Lance's mother, Barbara Hutton. (Wide World)

A Mouse reunion of sorts took place at Bobby Burgess' wedding to Kristie Floren on Valentine's Day, 1971. From left: Annette, husband, Jack, Dar-. lene Gillespie, Bobby, Kristie, Sharon Baird, Tommy Cole and wife, Aileen, Doreen Tracey and Bobby Diamond, an L.A. attorney, who—you may recall—once was the star of "Fury." (Courtesy Bobby Burgess)

Darlene Gillespie in a publicity shot for her new career as Darlene Valentine, country singer. (Alva Records)

BOWLES: Which of your pictures do you like best?

MOUSE: Unquestionably, it was *The Band Concert* which we did in 1935. That's the one, you'll remember, where I played the conductor and my sleeve kept falling down over my baton. Donald was really marvelous in that picture, distracting the band by playing a competing tune on his flute. That picture just had smashing visual effects.

BOWLES: From the standpoint of casting, since Pluto and Goofy were both dogs, how could one be your friend and equal and the other be your pet?

MOUSE: Well, I admit that does seem racist at this point in history. But you must remember that those pictures were made in the days before filmmakers began to be really conscious of oppressed minorities. Certainly, the attempt was simply to be funny and Mr. Disney meant no harm by it.

BOWLES: About your relationship with Walt Disney, Richard Schickel—

MOUSE: That's a sore subject with me.

BOWLES: —wrote a book called *The Disney Version*, which was not entirely charitable to either you or Mr. Disney.

MOUSE: Well, let me put it to you this way, the book—in addition to being somewhat malicious—had a number of really serious factual errors.

BOWLES: For example?

MOUSE: As you may know, Walt Disney had three brothers—Roy, who was a partner in the business; Herbert, who was a postman; and Ray. Schickel said that Ray had loaned Walt some money around 1930 which Walt had never paid back and their relationship ended there. That simply isn't true. Ray Disney handled the insurance for the company up until about 1947, I believe. He was around the studio almost every day in the early years.

BOWLES: What about—

MOUSE: Excuse me. In fact, there's a wonderful anecdote about Ray Disney which I'll tell you. When we were working on *Pinocchio*, the illustrators were stuck for a concept for the fox . . . J. Worthington Foulfellow. Everybody was sitting around all glum when the door opened and in walked Ray. He was a very colorful character with a flashy mustache; he always rode a bicycle too as I remember. Anyway, he walks in and Walt jumps up. "There's the sonofabitch now," he says. "That's our fox." So Ray Disney was the model for the fox.

BOWLES: What happened to him?

MOUSE: Well, some of the younger executives around the studio checked around and found out that we were just a little overinsured, shall we say, so we switched insurance companies. I think he retired from the business about then. He's still alive . . . lives over in Toluca Lake.

BOWLES: How did you get into the merchandising business?

MOUSE: That's an interesting story. In 1930, right after the first pictures really clicked, a company called Oregon Woolen Mills wrote to Mr. Roy Disney asking if they couldn't make a deal to put my picture on some products. The company always needed money in those days, so Roy struck a bargain with them for $1,000. Well, then he started getting offers from all over and he realized that he had made a mistake, so he bought the rights back.

BOWLES: Isn't that an illustration of what one businessman said: "The Disneys are always great on the honeymoon but six months later, when the house is in their name, they always want a divorce."

MOUSE: Well, I think that may be a bit harsh but it has some truth to it.

BOWLES: Is it true that your picture has appeared on more than five thousand products?

MOUSE: Well, yes. I think it may even be more than that. The character-merchandising end of the Disney operation really got into full swing about 1932 when a Mr. Kay Kamen approached Roy Disney about handling that end. Roy lied a little and said we were already doing more than $50,000 a year. Kamen said that was all right the company could keep the first $50,000 every year and he would split all above that fifty-fifty. That's the relationship that existed up until he was killed in a plane crash in 1949.

BOWLES: Do you have plans to make any pictures in the future?

MOUSE: Oh, I don't know. I suppose if the right part came along. There's too much violence in cartoons today. Do you ever watch those Saturday morning things? It's enough to warp a kid's mind. Also, the studio just isn't the same without Walt and Roy.

BOWLES: What do you mean?

MOUSE: Frankly, I think the new management is doing some things that Walt just wouldn't approve of. For example, this syndicated show called "The Mouse Factory." They chop the cartoons up to make them hip, like "Laugh-In" or something. Poor Walt is probably spinning like a top over that one. He never allowed the animated pictures to be chopped up like that. I don't think he'd like this "Disney on Parade" business very much either.

BOWLES: Are you saying that the new management is more conscious of creating new markets for Disney products than the Disneys were?

MOUSE: Yes, I'd say that. You can say many things about the Disneys but the fact is Walt was never particularly interested in money. He was interested in his pictures and in creating environments. If they made money that was fine but it was not his motivating force.

BOWLES: So you plan to stay in semiretirement?

MOUSE: Yes, I'm afraid that they just don't make pictures like they used to. Most of the pictures today are just, you know, too Mickey Mouse.

10

Doreen—
A Hollywood Child

Doreen Tracey's story begins halfway around the world from Hollywood in London, right in the middle of World War II. She was born there on April 13, 1943. To mark the occasion, the Fuehrer kept his air force home that night.

Doreen was, as they say, born to the stage. Her father, who died in 1970, was the youngest of a family of six Russian Jewish immigrants. His name was Murray Katzelnick but, of course, the Irish-American customs agent changed it to Murray Katz during the immigration process. Murray later returned the compliment by changing his name to Mickey Tracey. Murray was a hoofer and in those days times were hard for dancers with Jewish names. It was the season of the Irish, however, and Tracey served him just fine. Murray married his *shikse* dancing partner, Bessie, and put together an act that lasted through the Ziegfeld Follies right up until vaudeville's untimely end.

The big war was underway in Europe by then and there was still a demand for live shows, so the Traceys went off to Europe to entertain the troops. It was there, in the "burnt-out ends of smokey days," as Eliot once put it, that Doreen was born.

"We came back to the states when I was four," Doreen says, giving her head one of those girly flips. We are sitting in the cocktail lounge atop the Holiday Inn on North Highland and Hollywood Boulevard. The bar is called, for no apparent reason, Oscar's. The room rotates so that part of the time you're looking out on the Hollywood hills and the rest of the time the vista is downtown Los Angeles. As views go, it isn't much but the thought is nice.

"My father was very close to Ben Blue and they opened a place called Slappy Maxie on Wilshire. Then, I don't know, my mother got T.B. and had to go away for a while, so I lived with Uncle Ben—he's not my real uncle but he was that close and that's what I called him—in Beverly Hills.

"My father was busy just trying to stay afloat. He opened a dance studio called Rainbow Studio. It was nice and people like Debbie Reynolds studied there. I got a lot of free lessons."

Doreen lights a cigarette. She looks much the same as she did as a child—oversized eyes, a kind of saucer-shaped face, a quick and easy smile. She looks tired though and older than her thirty years. Clearly, there is mileage here and I feel a kind of inner sadness behind the laughing eyes.

Physically . . . well, Doreen was always the most physical of the Mouseketeers. Nature has endowed her with the kind of assets that men always notice. She is wearing a blue pants suit with a white turtle-neck sweater. She is the kind of girl for whom the sweater was invented. That Jane Russell "Us big girls have special problems" commercial passes briefly through my piggish mind.

"That's how I got into the Mouse Club," Doreen says. "I was never a great dancer or a great singer but because I had a terrific personality—and because Daddy owned the dance studio and could get them other kids—I got the job."

Doreen laughs warmly.

"I guess I was the real scatterbrain on the show. The other kids would tease me about that. But they really sheltered us so much on the show that we weren't prepared to face the life outside. That kind of thing warps your personality so that you can't handle the reality thing. I mean, it's a fantastic world but there are more dimensions to it than just Hollywood . . . thank God for that."

She glances at her watch.

"I can't stay too long," she says. "I have a cousin visiting from New York. Checking up on me, I suppose. I'm doing fine, really."

I wait for Doreen to explain but she has obviously decided she's said too much already. It is one of several mysterious, oblique references in our conversation. The talk shifts to Annette.

"I think Annette was the most salable product Disney had at that time. In those days, the whole Italian ethnic thing was hot and she was kind of a small version of your Sophia Loren or Gina Lollobrigida who were the top box office stars at that moment.

"The timing was perfect and, besides, she was good. Look, if I had to choose I'd put my money on a personality any day instead of a talent. Ten thousand people may be good dancers, but if they don't have that certain identity, that certain magnetism, that people identify with . . . then it doesn't help them a bit.

"Annette stood out. She had that little extra bit of charisma that made you look at her and that's what sells. That's commercial. Most of us were out there hamming it up but Annette never overacted and that's what drew your attention to her.

"I mean, Darlene was probably the most talented and gifted of the group but she was a little puppet. She wasn't real. I'd put my money on Annette any day."

"What did you think of Disney?" I ask. It is a question I ask all the former Mouseketeers with some widely varying responses.

"He was a jerk," Doreen says, then bursts out laughing. "No, really. I think he was a good man and a genius. The only sort of human thing I remember about him is one time when Annette and I were about fourteen and they used to make us wear those bloody T-shirts under our Mouse sweaters so that we would be flattened down. We were both very big-chested broads, really top heavy for fourteen-year-olds. We used to slash the T-shirts down the middle so our breasts would stick through. Anyway, we were walking down the lot one day and we passed Disney and a couple of other guys. One of them said "Look, aren't the girls growing up?" and Disney said "Girls? They're more for the fathers than the kids in the audience."

* * *

The scene at the Sydney airport is unbelievable. Ten thousand Australian teen-agers shouting and screaming and waving signs, surging forward toward the plane carrying Jimmie Dodd and the Mouseketeer tour. The year is 1959 and until The Beatles venture down under in 1966, it is the biggest show biz mob scene ever. Although this isn't an "official" Mouseketeer tour (meaning Disney didn't organize or finance it), that point is lost on the adoring Aussies. For some reason—perhaps because of the spirit of the show—the "Mickey Mouse Club" held a place of special affection in the hearts of Australians. It ran there in syndication for fourteen years, longer than anywhere else in the world.

As the plane taxis up to the gate, the enthusiastic crowd pushes forward. Jimmie Dodd comes down first and somebody hands him a koala bear which—in the excitement of the moment—scratches him on the face. Jimmie stands there bleeding and grinning and saying "Gee, isn't he cute," and his wife Ruth dabs at the cut with a handkerchief and Bobby and Sharon come down the steps.

Suddenly, the crowd goes completely quiet. All eyes swing toward a fantastic creature descending the steps.

It is Doreen. Not the cute little Doreen they remembered from the Mouse Club but a seventeen-year-old, all grown up in all the right places, Doreen with flaming red hair, tight blue jeans, and a hot pink T-shirt that looks like it just might collapse from exhaustion at any moment. For the puritanical Australians (in 1959 the bars closed at 6 P.M. and *Playboy* was not allowed in the country), it is a truly liberating moment.

"I loved it, of course," Doreen says. "The newspapers were filled with these Mouseketeer sexpot stories. I couldn't walk down the street because boys would follow me and try to touch me and the police would have to come and rescue me.

"I had a mad, torrid affair going at the time with Dave Summerville, the lead singer of The Diamonds, and I used to get drunk in the lounge with Dave and that got into the papers and was bad."

"What happened with the Dave thing?"

"Mother broke it up," Doreen says, without malice. "Poor darling, she almost had a heart attack over it. I used to sneak out and see him anyway . . . but it just got too difficult after a while."

Doreen does one of those innocent, coy things with her eyes. She is very sexy. Annette and Darlene may have gotten more exposure on the Mouse Club but Doreen was not without her following. The New York *Mirror*, may it rest in peace, reported on June 23, 1957, that it had been inundated by pleas to run pictures of Mouseketeers. "A typical request," the article said, "came from a very junior miss whose parents named her Arlette Gaines, of Glen Oaks, Long Island. However, she insists upon being called 'Doreen' after her favorite Doreen Tracey. 'Arlette, I mean Doreen, won't even answer unless you call her by her new name,' her mother, Mrs. Thomas Gaines explained sadly."

* * *

After the Australian tour, Doreen went back to John Burroughs High School in Burbank where she met and fell in love with a "Robert Redford" type named Robert Washburn. Although they were both teen-agers, they ran off to Tijuana and got married. Shortly thereafter, Doreen got pregnant.

Marriage was not Doreen's thing, however (nor was it Lonnie Burr's or Sharon Baird's).

"We were friendly with Lonnie Burr then and he and Bobby used to hang around together a little. I had my son—Bradley Allen Washburn—but I couldn't take being married. One day I called up Cheryl and said I didn't dig this being married business and I was getting a divorce. So I did. My son is twelve now and he's just great."

"What is your ex-husband now?" I ask.

"He's a reformed drug addict," Doreen says. "At least I hope he's reformed."

Doreen looks wistful, stares into her glass. She seems on the edge of telling me something but the moment passes.

"You could get drunk up here," she says, "with this thing moving around." She lights a cigarette. "You know, I think you're a lot better friends with Lonnie than you let on."

"Why do you say that?"

"I dunno," she says. "I just think so."

The conversation shifts to Cheryl Holdridge, the ex-Mouseketeer with whom Doreen has remained most friendly over the years.

"I was a bridesmaid at Cheryl's wedding to Lance Reventlow," she says. "That wedding. It was a real Cecil B. DeMille production. I was a blonde at the time and Cheryl made we wear this awful wig because she was a blonde and she didn't want me to clash. But she really loved Lance and he really loved her."

Doreen pushes her hair back with an ultra girly gesture.

"I'll tell you how much she loved him," Doreen says. "We were hostesses at a magazine promotion party once and in walks Lance. Cheryl says to me: 'See that guy? He used to be married to Jill St. John.' 'So?' I say. 'Well,' she says, 'I'm in love with him and I'm going to be married to him within a year.' 'Oh, come on,' I say. Sure enough, about a year later, Cheryl calls one day and says, 'Guess who I'm getting married to?' It was Lance."

Doreen keeps talking but my mind has stopped at the idea of "hostesses." Being seen at the right parties was part of the whole starlet bit in the 1950s. It still is, for that matter. What better way to spice up a promotion party than to hire a few unattached beauties to stand around and look decorative. God knows it's a way of making important contacts for the girls. That's show biz.

"I don't know," Doreen says. "I just felt funny about the whole situation. Maybe I just had a sixth sense about what was going to happen to Lance."

Doreen remained fairly active professionally during the early 1960s. Like Tommy Cole, she performed with the Andressi Brothers in Las Vegas and elsewhere, appeared on shows like "Donna Reed," "Day in Court," and "My Three Sons," and put together her own nightclub act in which she sang and danced and did impressions of people like Streisand, Carol Channing, Lena Horne, and Ann-Margret. With the USO, she toured Alaska and the Orient.

"What's the wildest thing you ever did?" I ask, taking a stab in the dark.

"I shot a guy once in Vietnam," she says.

"You what?" I say, making a mental note to stop drinking.

"I shot this black guy in Vietnam. He grabbed me and tried to rape me and I got hold of his .45 and shot him. His friend came and dragged him out and I really don't know what happened. It was hushed up and I never heard any more about it."

Doreen returned to the states in 1968 and has sworn off show business for good, she says. She's been working as an administrative assistant at Warner Brothers Records and "learning the business."

"I have to go soon," Doreen says. "My cousin, you know."

Doreen sips the remains of her drink.

"I really envy Annette," she says, suddenly pensive. "I wish I had the kind of contentment she has . . . just to be with one guy and the kids and all. I really envy all that. Wouldn't it be great if we could all live in that funny little world forever?

"But the Mouseketeers," she says. "I think the whole group is a bore. We're all bores. The last time we got together I just sat there and said to myself . . . oh, shit."

* * *

A few months later I called Doreen to ask her to send me some pictures for the book. She seemed very excited.

"I've gotten involved with Synanon," she says. "It's changed my life. It's the most wonderful thing. Do you know about it?"

"Isn't that the drug rehabilitation group?" I say.

"Sure is."

She asked me to be sure and say something about Synanon in the book. I promised that I would.

11

Karen and Cubby

The 1950s was a decade of couples. Eddie and Debbie. Tommy and Nancy. Mike and Liz. Bob and Natalie. Frankie and Annette. Certain people were just destined for each other. At least, it seemed that way.

Karen and Cubby were Hollywood's youngest and, in many ways, most perfect couple. Everybody was sure that they would grow up and get married and live happily ever after.

Because they were younger than the other Mouseketeers and the same age (To be exact, Karen is thirteen days older. She was born on July 1, 1946, in Glendale; Cubby was born on July 14 in Burbank.), they spent most of their time together.

Cubby, who was a half year ahead of Karen in school, even held back a term just so he could be in the same class. They took dancing lessons and riding lessons and swimming lessons together.

David Stollery, who played Marty on "Spin & Marty," a terrific artist who grew up to be one of Detroit's better automobile designers, even drew a picture of the house they would live in when they grew up. Karen still has it . . . somewhere.

"I didn't see Cubby much after the show ended," Karen says, sinking into the sofa with an energetic bounce. "I'm not sure why." She smiles. She and her husband, Michael DeLauer, a lawyer, had just moved into a new house in the Toluca Lake section of North Hollywood the day before and I am here at an obviously awkward moment. Painters are doing the walls and furniture is scattered everywhere. Her white cat, Miracle, wanders through with a confused look on his face.

Despite all, Karen has dressed up for my visit. She is wearing a stunning black velvet pantsuit and a white blouse with ruffles and is as cute as the day she stepped onto the Mouseketeer set. She still has the long, strawberry-blond hair and a contagious giggle.

"I guess I last saw Cubby a couple of years ago," she says. "I meant to go to his wedding but I got the dates all mixed up. I even got dressed and called to find out directions and they said 'that was last week.' I do things like that all the time." She giggles. I giggle. Miracle jumps in my lap.

"Did you go to Cheryl's wedding?" I ask.

"No," she says. "I wasn't invited. I didn't go to Annette's either. I was invited to that one. I just didn't go." She sighs. "I don't know. . . . I just always felt funny around those people after I left the show. They never treated me bad or anything like that. But, it's just the way I am. I never had any confidence in myself."

There is something distinctly un-show bizzy about Karen and, despite the fact that her father was a Hollywood set builder, her emergence as a star on the "Mickey Mouse Club" was mostly an accident. Her dance teacher, Elaine Troy, took her with two other students to one of the open auditions for the show. Karen, who was eight at the time, had absolutely no idea what was going on but when she was asked to sing and dance, she did, charming producer Bill Walsh and the others. It probably didn't hurt that Jimmie Dodd recognized her from Sunday school at his church, the First Presbyterian Church of North Hollywood.

"A few days later they called my mother and told her to take me down to the office there, you know, where you get the work permits and I was on the show," she says. "I still didn't have much of an idea what was going on." Karen wrinkles her nose at her naïveté.

"This is really funny," she says. "When we started filming the first day, I didn't know about film and all that stuff. I thought we were live and I had to do it right the first time. The first time Dick Darley yelled cut, I thought to myself 'Gee, that man is crazy. Doesn't he know we're on television?'"

Karen was never close to the older girls and was mostly unaware of the intense, and often bitter, rivalry that was going on between Annette and Darlene and their respective parents. When Bronson Scott and Linda Hughes and Sherry Alberoni (then known as Sherry Allen) came, she had friends her own age. But for the first year or so, she and Cubby were inseparable. She was the darling of several of the adults, though. Roy Williams threw a birthday party for her at his house when she turned nine.

"I remember they had a birthday cake with nine candles on it and they floated it around the pool on a board. My mother made a tape of everybody saying 'Happy Birthday, Karen.' I still have it . . . somewhere."

Karen's big thing on the show—other than looking cute which was easy—was a song called "Gee, But It's Hard to Be Eight." She sang it until she was twelve. She also did a short bit called "Karen in Cartoonland" and introduced the Annette series: "And now, the 'Mickey Mouse Club' proudly presents . . . Annette."

"Did you get to know Walt Disney?" I ask.

Karen flashes a shy grin, like somebody who is about to make a startling confession.

"I don't know if I'm allowed to say this or not," she says.

I lean forward to hear the forbidden secret.

"Well," Karen says, tentatively, "I got the impression he didn't like kids very much." For a moment, I had the distinct impression that Karen was half expecting a flash of lightning to descend through the roof of her pretty new house. "He was never very friendly. I loved Bill Walsh . . . and Sidney Miller, he was great. He used to do things that were just hysterical. Like one time we were doing this One-a-Day vitamin commercial and, you know how you sometimes get the giggles, I kept breaking up everytime I was supposed to say the line. By the thirty-second take, Sid Miller was down on the floor, sobbing and pounding the floor with his fist, and screaming 'Please do it right. Please.' He was real funny like that. He was sometimes gruff but he always came around later to make up. And like he was always doing silly things like stuffing cigarettes up his nose . . . stuff like that."

* * *

Northridge is a twenty-minute ride on the Hollywood Freeway from Toluca Lake. Cubby O'Brien lives there with his wife, Marilyn, a singer, and his four-year-old daughter, Alicia. He hasn't seen Karen in, gee, it's been a long time.

Cubby has grown a foot since his Mouse days and now stands in at a towering five feet six. The crew cut is gone now and he sports a dapper little mustache.

"I guess I'd have to say I'm a positive on the subject of the Mouse Club," he says. "My whole career developed out of that so I have no regrets about it."

And, in fact, Cubby has managed to keep more constructively busy in show business than many of the others. This is undoubtedly due to the fact that he is a musician, and a good one, and not an actor.

Cubby comes by his musical training rather naturally. His father, Haskel "Hack" O'Brien, was a well-known drummer with bands like Paul Whiteman and Tommy Dorsey in the thirties and forties. He started teaching Cubby when he was six.

By the age of eight, Cubby was the youngest member of the Roger Babcock Dixieland Band. Roger Babcock's father owned the music studio where "Hack" O'Brien taught.

One of the Disney producers—Cubby forgets which one—saw him playing at the Screen Actors Guild and invited him to audition for the Mouse Club. Two auditions after that, he was hired and became the youngest Mouseketeer.

The Disney people figured him to be one of the most popular Mouseketeers which, in fact, he was. Even today, he is the one most people remember after Annette. Cubby was a terrific drummer then. He still is.

After the Mouse Club, Cubby went straight to the "Lawrence Welk Show" for two years. Unlike Bobby who stayed, Cubby's experience there was less than fortuitous.

"I don't know how much I want to say about it," Cubby says, "but I couldn't get into the Welk show. I mean, he was a nice man and all that but I just didn't fit in, in the right way. I got the feeling that you were expected to be all for the show and I just wasn't up for that. It was a big family and, well frankly, I also had the feeling that it was important to be a Catholic. That may have changed now. After all, I'm talking about fifteen years ago. But, then, it seemed important."

After Welk, Cubby formed his own group for a while, continued to attend Hollywood Professional School, and then went on the road with the Spike Jones Band for a couple of years.

"We did mostly a lounge act in Vegas and Tahoe," Cubby says. "Spike's a nice man and I got a lot of important experience playing show music. You can't always play jazz or rock or the stuff you like in this business."

It was Ann-Margret who was most instrumental in helping Cubby get into studio work, a tough but lucrative business for those who are lucky enough to get the few available jobs. Ann-Margret once paid off Shelly Manne, who had been hired to work with her in five shows, in order to keep Cubby as her drummer. If you know anything about drumming, that's a hell of a recommendation.

Cubby has done more and more contract work over the years with Jim Nabors and, most particularly, Carol Burnett. Lately, he's been so busy doing television and nightclub work with The Carpenters that he now shares his duties on the "Carol Burnett Show" with another drummer.

"I've also done some conducting," he says. "I was John Davidson's conductor for a while and I was musical director of the L.A. productions of *Hair* and *Oh! Calcutta!* Looks like everytime a dirty show comes to town, they call me up."

During our talk, Cubby asks about some of the other ex-

Mouseketeers whom he doesn't see often. I told him about Darlene's new recording career.

"That's great," he says. "I'm really glad to hear that."

"I guess, next to you, of course, she was the most talented person on the show," I say.

"She was the most talented . . . including me," Cubby says. "Something happened at Disney that turned her off to the business for a long, long time."

"What?"

"I think she ought to tell you."

"You're talking about the fact that the studio pushed Annette."

"Yes."

Cubby has been married for eight years. He met Marilyn, who was then a member of a group called the Goodtime Singers, while touring with Spike Jones.

"I really don't know what happened with Karen," he says. "She just sort of dropped out of the business after the Mouse Club and I never saw her. It was never a romantic thing between us anyway, although I think a lot of people thought—or hoped—it was."

Cubby doesn't remember the picture of the dream house that David Stollery drew.

*   *   *

After the MMC ended, Karen went back to school and lived, she says, "a normal, everybody life." Like most of the Mouseketeers who returned to public school, the going was tough at first . . . particularly accentuated by the years of extreme protectiveness at the Disney studio. Kids would ask Karen for her autograph and then tear it up while she watched. Or they would say things like "Wiggle your ears and I'll give you some cheese." Eventually, though, the Mouseketeer fame wore off.

Although she seldom saw Cubby after the show ended, Karen occasionally went out with another ex-Mouseketeer named Johnny Crawford—"a really nice boy" as Karen puts it. Crawford has had one of the most interesting show biz careers of any of the ex-Mouseketeers. He costarred on "The Rifleman" for five seasons, has had records in the top ten, been a professional rodeo cowboy, and just recently got his first movie starring role in *The Naked Ape,* a film with enough exposed flesh to send Walt Disney spinning in his grave or in that block of ice that some people say he had himself frozen in. Crawford's picture—totally, full frontally nude—appeared in the Christmas 1973 issue of *Playboy* in an article called "Sex Stars of 1973." He, thus, joins Dennis Day, who confessed to his bisexuality in *Rolling Stone,* as ex-Mouseketeers that one suspects the Disney organization would just as soon forget about.

But, that's another story.

After high school, Karen went to San Fernando College for a year and a half but quit because, she says, "I really couldn't get into college very much. I guess I never really liked school that much anyway."

She quit school and got a job at the May Company department store as a sales clerk in the toy department.

"I was so embarrassed one day," she says, lighting a cigarette. "Cheryl came in. 'Karen, how are you?' she says. She was married to Lance Reventlow then. Here she was in all these diamonds and things and there was little old me . . . a sales clerk at May Company. We talked a while and she picked up this model of a boat and said, 'I'm going to buy this because it's exactly like one Lance and I have.'"

Karen smiles, a bit sadly this time, I think.

"Then—let's see—then I got a job at Prudential. This girlfriend came by and said she was going down to Prudential to interview for a job and asked if I would like to come along. I said sure, you know, because May Company doesn't pay that much. She's since got married and moved to Alaska or something like that, but I'm still there.

"It's a job. It's something to do. You don't have to know anything or do anything. I'm a clerk in the mortgage loan department . . . a special clerk, but still a clerk. They have these dumb little titles they pass around.

"We get free lunch and free parking, though," she says.

Karen made her last show business appearance nearly four years ago, just before she got married, when she appeared as a man-seeking bachelorette on the TV show "The Dating Game." By the time the producers called her to appear, she was already engaged to Mike DeLauer but she decided to appear anyway.

"It was a research game," she explains. "Bobby Burgess was one of the guys. I recognized his voice the minute he said hello. I remember being so relieved that I wouldn't have to go out with somebody I didn't know. But I played along and asked all the dumb questions and acted like I was thinking about it.

"We went to Lake Tahoe and had a lot of fun, really. We danced a lot. . . . I love to dance and so does Bobby . . . and we really had a good time. Bobby was already engaged to Kristie by then too."

Karen married DeLauer, whom she had known for seven years, in 1970. None of the Mouseketeers came to her wedding. Mike had just come back from thirteen months with the Marines in Vietnam. Karen had written a letter every day.

"At the time, I was all for the war, you know," she says. "After all, if my boyfriend was there, there had to be something to it. Right? Now I say, forget it. Boy, was I dumb. I guess I had to be the true-blue all-American girlfriend, though."

"Do you miss being in show business?" I say, over the sound of a carpenter fixing the back door with a hammer.

"No," she says, after a moment of reflection. "Oh, I guess when I go to a big musical I want to get in there and do it . . . but I'm not sure that I could, even if I wanted to. I'm happy now. . . . I did almost get a job in Vegas once as a dancer. I was too short."

She pauses to light another cigarette. The afternoon sun pours through the curtainless window, playing with her golden pink curls.

"Dancing was my number-one thing," she says. "I was in *Westward Ho* but acting is not really for me. Sometimes now, even when I go to the Ice Follies, I want to be an Ice Capades person.

"And, like when I watch the Academy Awards, I get all misty

and think, imagine me winning the Academy Award and walking up there and saying thanks. I get over it after a while, though."

The smile fades slowly.

"I don't always agree with the Academy Awards, anyway. I was a little disappointed in *The Godfather*. I read the book and thought it was great. I waited for the movie to come out. And, like, I don't read that much. I read *The Robe* once and it took me two years. I mostly read Sherlock Holmes. He's my favorite."

Karen goes on to say that she likes Jerry Lewis pictures and Disney movies which are "always entertaining and kind of dumb."

"What do you think of the 'Mickey Mouse Club' in retrospect?" I ask.

"I think it was a really great kids' show," she says. "And I'm not just bragging because I was on it or anything. I know people who named their kids after people on the show. I think it was good because there were real people, not just a bunch of cartoons. I like cartoons, myself, but it's better to have people to identify with. It was goody-goody, for sure, but all of the Disney stuff is like that. I'm sure the show had a strong effect on the people who watched it."

The telephone rings and Karen goes to answer it. A house painter, a young guy with longish hair who has been listening throughout, wanders over to the coffee table and picks up a picture of Karen in her Mouseketeer costume.

"Mickey Mouse," he says, in a perfect Donald Duck voice. "Far freakin' out."

12

Jimmie

The big Mouseketeer has appeared. Jimmie, an older man
who wears circular black ears. Rabbit watches him atten-
tively; he respects him. He expects to learn something from
him helpful in his own line of work, which is demonstrating a
kitchen gadget in several five-and-dime stores around Brewer.
He's had the job for four weeks. "Proverbs, proverbs, they're
so true," Jimmie sings, strumming his Mouseguitar, "proverbs
tell us what to do. Proverbs help us all to bee—better—
Mouse-ke-teers."

JOHN UPDIKE, *Rabbit Run*, 1960

If the "Mickey Mouse Club" had a lasting spirit, if it truly
touched the heart of a generation, the reason was a friendly red-
headed, freckle-faced man named Jimmie Dodd. Jimmie was good
and he wore his goodness like a banner. He wrote many of the
songs for the show and all of the "Doddisms"—petite morality lessons for the young. Jimmie did have one small vanity. His age.
When Walt Disney knighted him chief Mouseketeer in 1955,
Jimmie was forty-five years old. He told *TV Guide* he was thirty-
four. It's a small thing, really, and God probably didn't mind.

Jimmie was born in Cincinnati and his show business career before the MMC had been less than illustrious. Band jobs in high
school and college; a singing job for a St. Petersburg, Florida,
radio station; bit parts in a number of movies including the 1944
Abbott and Costello epic *Buck Privates Come Home*; a number
of USO tours with his wife Ruth Carroll, a dancer; and a winning
appearance on Arthur Godfrey's "Talent Scouts."

He was a prolific songwriter, turning out more than four hundred in his lifetime. These included such songs as "Nashville
Blues," "Rosemary," "I Love Girls," and "Mamie," a song written
in 1952 in honor of Mrs. Dwight D. Eisenhower.

Ruth Dodd, who is now married to Harold Braun, an L.A. ac-
countant, agrees to meet me for lunch to talk about her late husband. Ruth is a handsome, matronly woman, very sweet and
pleasant. I began by telling Ruth that I felt the MMC was more
the spirit of Jimmie Dodd than Walt Disney.

"Did you know that he was a Christian?" she says.

I said I knew he was active in the church.

"Well, not only active in the church," Ruth says. "This was
definitely in his life. He was a born-again Christian and he tried to
get this kind of message across in everything he did."

Ruth orders a grilled cheese on rye and coffee. I choose a
reuben sandwich and a Coke. Ordinarily, I would have had a
reuben sandwich and a Coor's but the "born-again Christian"
comment, a phrase I hadn't heard since I was a boy in the funda-
mental backwoods of West Virginia, already has me on the defen-
sive. Religious words always make me feel guilty for some reason
or another.

"The early producer of the show . . . I wish I could think of
his name. Isn't this terrible. He had a good deal to do with allow-
ing Jimmie to use his own ideas in the show."

"Was that Hal Adelquist?"

"Right. He was a real strong influence in the beginning but
then, of course, he had his problems and left the studio."

Ruth avoids saying what Adelquist's problems were but I sug-
gest that Hal, perhaps, drank more than he should have.

Sharon Baird was—and still is—the most outgoing Mouseketeer. She appears in several Sid and Marty Kroft children's television productions.

The horseperson is the same in both pictures. At top, Doreen Tracey displays good form at age six. Bottom, she shows even better form at twenty-five. (Courtesy Doreen Tracey)

Johnny Crawford revealed all in the movie The Naked Ape, *a 1972 turkey from Playboy Productions.* (UPI)

Remember little Sherry Allen, the smallest Mouseketeer? Well, her real name is Sherry Alberoni—apparently somebody in casting thought the Club was top heavy with Italians because they also changed Don Agrati to Don Grady. Sherry is an actress specializing in voice characterizations for TV cartoon shows like "The Partridge Family." She is married to Dr. Richard Van Meter, a physician, and has a daughter. (Courtesy Sherry Alberoni)

"Yes. It was very bad and it ruined a man who had a very wonderful feel and who had a real spiritual feel if he had only allowed himself to overcome this. But I know from the contact that Jim and I had with him that he really encouraged Jim and wanted him to use his ideas because he knew how Jim felt about the Lord. He was very helpful in getting as much of this into the show as he could because, after all, it was a secular show. It was not that kind of show so they had to play it very carefully."

Ruth smiles sweetly.

"I don't know how familiar you are with Jim's life story before he came to Disney, but he had a very serious illness in 1951 that the doctors actually gave him up. He was in Hollywood Presbyterian Hospital. He, of course, couldn't get into the service in World War II because he had a badly damaged heart valve. He had a very enlarged heart and a murmur. He got a strep infection and after five and a half weeks of not responding to medicine they said they thought they were going to have to let him go home and we thought maybe they meant that would be the end. And they said if he doesn't respond to medicine at home we think maybe you should turn him over to the county as a test case because, I mean, financially we were wiped out. I had to give him shots around the clock every four hours. . . . We began to get letters from all around the country. Jim had been in pictures and had a pretty good audience built up and they were writing saying we're praying for Jim.

"And we felt that it was the prayers that pulled him through because after months of being home he wrote that song which won the contest for a song about Washington, D.C. He saw it advertised in *Billboard*. He wrote the song and won, which meant $1,000 for him."

The Washington song provided an important boost for Dodd who, Ruth says, had been somewhat discouraged as a songwriter. He had written one very big hit called "Rosemary" during World War II, but times had been hard after that. Only two months after his near-fatal illness Jimmie and Ruth were honored in Washington for his song.

The next year, Jinx Falkenberg—with whom the Dodds had toured on a USO show during the war—invited Jimmie to appear on her show in New York. While there, she suggested that he appear on "Arthur Godfrey's Talent Scouts" program. He was not thrilled with the idea in the beginning since he felt he had too many years in the business to start over again on what was essentially an amateur show. He was finally convinced that the show would provide important coverage, appeared, and won. It gave his career a new boost, at least for a while.

"We went back to New York to do Jinx' show two different summers but—you know how it is in this town—if you're not around and up for things you're soon forgotten. And, too, television was just coming in and a lot of that work was in New York. Jimmie had managed to keep us alive by working in pictures, nothing big, really, but enough to keep us going, but they weren't making as many pictures. So, we were really scrounging."

The food arrives at this point.

"I don't know if you say 'thanks' or not but I'd like to," Ruth says.

"Go ahead," I say, instinctively looking around to see who's going to notice. Nobody does.

"Father we thank you for your many blessings. We thank you for this opportunity to share something that may be meaningful. In Jesus' name. Amen."

Ruth sips her coffee.

"We were invited to go to this Hollywood Christian group which is a group for anybody in the business . . . this is by preface to the Disney thing. On Monday nights they would have meetings and we started to go. Oh, we knew about God and we even went to a church which we later found out was not a Christ-centered church but, I guess, what you would call a cult nowadays. And at the Hollywood Christian group we found out for the first time that we could only have a true relationship with God through Jesus Christ. . . . We finally began learning that this was the real answer to our life. . . . But through Christ, we had a real cleansing of all of our sins and we also had the promise of eternal life and we thought, wow, this is the answer to all our problems.

"So when we came back to this town and all the doors were closed to us, we actually prayed together for the first time. We asked the Lord if he wanted Jim not to be in show business to shut every door so tight . . . and this was all he knew, really. We got down on our knees and we said we'll both be willing to do whatever you want us to do.

"And the next day—this was the miracle in our life—a good friend who was a director over at Disney that Jim played a lot of tennis with—Jim would never ask one of his friends for a job—this friend called and said that Walt wants a song about a pencil because without the pencil there wouldn't be Mickey Mouse and there wouldn't be this studio."

Jimmie, as it happened, wrote best on assignment and he quickly dashed off a pencil song and made a demo record. His friend—Bill Justus—managed to get Disney to listen to it and Jimmie was hired as a songwriter by the studio. He was given an office and allowed to write for cartoons and for "Disneyland-TV," the nighttime show.

"Walt would come up to his office and say, 'I'm pretty tired today, Jim. Why don't you sing some of your new things?' This was just fantastic because Walt knew his work."

Dodd, as it turned out, was the perfect choice for emcee. He had instant rapport with kids, although he and Ruth had never had any of their own. He was modestly talented as a singer but could turn out songs at the drop of an idea and he was totally charming, in a slightly saccharine sort of way. But, he was sincere, even the most cynical ex-Mouseketeer will grant you that, and his sincerity came through. Jimmie's entire life, it seems in retrospect, was pointed toward being the chief Mouseketeer of the "Mickey Mouse Club."

"Have you seen many of the kids?" Ruth asks.

I said I had.

"Annette is a beautiful girl, inside and out," she says. "And Bobby. He's my kid."

I told Ruth that I had never heard a consensus about an individual in the way people who knew him seemed to feel about Jimmie.

"He was pretty terrific," she says. "I was married to him twenty-four years and I ought to know."

As the show went into production, Ruth became more involved in the operations also. One of the most memorable production numbers—"Cooking with Minnie Mouse"—was her idea. She also coauthored some of Jim's songs, the best known of these being a spiritual number called "Do What the Good Book Says."

After the show ended, Ruth and Jim led Mouseketeer tours to Australia in 1959 and 1960. He continued to make personal appearances and work with Disney until 1964 when he was invited to come to Hawaii to put together a children's TV show.

"After the first day of filming there," Ruth says, "he went into the hospital and was there three months then passed away. But we got enough in that one day of shooting, with me working and using a stand-in, for thirteen weeks. Isn't that fantastic?

"If I hadn't belonged to the Lord, I think I would have flipped when Jim was ill because for those three months the television station had so much money wrapped up in this. They had bought a video tape recorder just for our show. We were the first show ever actually made right there in Hawaii. . . . Now, they're doing a lot. Anyway they had hoped to sell the show all over the world; just like the Mouseketeer show had an audience, they hoped this would have too.

"When Jim was taken to the hospital so ill . . . he was hit by a staph infection and had to have so much medication, the studio said don't let anybody know that he's in the hospital or that he's ill. We had a couple of big commercials—a bread sponsor and a milk sponsor—we just didn't dare let it be known.

"I had to go back to the hotel and to tell everybody that he's doing great and it broke my heart knowing how really serious it was.

"Jim had a mother and an aunt—he was an only child—and they were back here in California and we finally had to tell them that he was in the hospital because they were wondering why they weren't getting any mail from him. He couldn't write, you know, because his arms were down like this with all those tubes and things in them.

"So every Saturday I would go to the hospital and we'd put in a call and he talked to them and they thought he was coming along all right . . . but I finally had to tell them how serious it was and they came out and were there for the last month.

"But," Ruth says, her eyes becoming more sad, "that man had such a spirit. All the people at the hospital loved him and he would witness to his doctors, to the nurses, to the little cleaning lady who came in his room. This guy was unbelievable, even as he was suffering terribly, and died right under our eyes, he had such a spirit."

Ruth gives me a fervent look.

"How about you?" she says after a moment. "Do you know the Lord Jesus Christ as your Savior?"

I had to admit I didn't and quickly changed the subject. I asked Ruth what she thought the "Mickey Mouse Club" meant to the kids who watched it.

"I think it was something very special," she says, "and it wasn't just all Jim, although he had a lot to do with it. Walt had this idea. He didn't like the kinds of things that were being shoved at kids in those days. He wanted to do something different. There were a lot of people motivated to do something by his idea. One time a little stewardess came up to Jim on a plane and said she was a stewardess because she had seen a feature about that on the 'Mickey Mouse Club.' So many things like that happened over the years. It was very special. So was Jim."

13

Sharon

If there were any justice in show business, which there isn't, Sharon Baird would be a star. Sharon was the littlest Mouseketeer, standing in at a whopping four feet, eight inches tall, which is exactly two inches shorter than she is today. She was the best dancer of the group, had had the most show biz experience before arriving at the Mouse Club, and had the most energy and enthusiasm. She was, or so it seemed at the time, a natural performer.

Shortness seems to be a characteristic that all the red team Mouseketeers—with the exception of Bobby, who is about six feet tall—share. Perhaps, the reason is that in the 1950s diminutive and cute meant the same thing, and producers selected child performers on the basis of their cuteness. This, of course, causes problems for people in the acting business because cute kids most often grow up to be cute adults and there isn't much market for cute adults in movies these days. Most of the Mouseketeers are short people and, as silly as it may seem, it is a bond between them.

There is another shared characteristic which is more difficult to explain. The overwhelming majority of Mouseketeers still live in the San Fernando Valley. If you took a compass, put its point on Burbank, and swung it in a fifty-mile radius, you would have en-

circled the hometowns of a good 80 per cent of the ex-Mouseketeers. I'm not sure exactly why that is except, perhaps, to say that
the middle class is a lifestyle from which few escape.

Sharon lives in Sherman Oaks, a pleasant little community not
too far out in the Valley, in a kind of fairy-tale house. Not that
it's a castle or anything, far from it, but the house seems to have
been built for someone of her small stature.

"Look," Sharon says, standing on her tippytoes, "I can reach all
the cabinets." She can, too. We are having coffee in her living
room, while a radio drones rock music gently in the background.
The house is furnished in shopping center modern and there are
several "cute" books lying around. (Cute, you know, like a category of books. Charlie Brown. Snoopy. That sort of thing.)

I'm confused about Sharon. Although I see her several times I
always come away thinking we never really talked at all. She is aggressively good-natured in a way that annoys cynical people like
myself. She always, always answers her phone by saying "Yes, in-
deedy!"

Our first meeting is straight out of a Laurel and Hardy movie.
She is in New York as part of a tour production of Sid and Marty
Krofft's television series "H. R. Pufnstuf." Sharon appears on the
show, as well as other Krofft productions like "Lidsville" and
"Bugaloo." These are kids shows which are on, on Saturday
morning. Sharon dresses up like an owl and does dances and
things like that.

It wasn't always that way.

Sharon was born in Seattle on August 16, 1943. Her father
worked for Boeing. He was a handy man to have around in the
aircraft industry since he was only five feet two, and could crawl
up into wings and other tight spots. Sharon started taking dancing
lessons at the age of three and by five she was already making appearances at the Palomar Theatre in Seattle with people like the
Ink Spots and the Hoosier Hot Shots.

When she was seven, Sharon won the "Little Miss Washington" contest and the prize was a two-week expense-paid trip to
Los Angeles to compete in the "Little Miss U.S.A." contest.

"My mother fell in love with California," Sharon says, with a smile that is always just on the verge of breaking into a giggle. She has sort of reddish hair and is as cute as a bug, as they say. "When we went back, she told my father how much she liked it and he said, okay, so he quit his job at Boeing which he had had for ten years and we moved down. He got a job working for Flying Tiger Airlines and I started studying with Louis de Pron and looking for work."

She didn't have to look that hard. Eddie Cantor took a liking to this happy little kid and signed her to a contract to appear on "The Colgate Comedy Hour." Cantor had already signed a cute little blond-haired boy named Lonnie Burr.

Sharon became quite popular in a look-Martha-isn't-that-cute sort of way. She was even awarded the ultimate accolade for a dancer. Her legs were insured for $50,000 with Lloyd's of London. Not in the Mitzi Gaynor tax bracket, of course, but not bad for a kid.

After Cantor's heart attack and the folding of the show, she cast about for work. She found several movie jobs and knew about the auditions for the Mouseketeers. Her agent—she was one of the few kids to have one—was dead set against her working for Disney, feeling, with some justification, that she could make more money elsewhere. But, there is something that does not love a Hollywood agent, and fate intervened.

Sharon had been cast in a Martin and Lewis picture called *Artists and Models* and was at Capitol Records one day prerecording a song for the picture. She chanced upon one Jimmie Dodd who was also there recording a song. Jimmie, who knew a good prospect when he saw one, invited her to come out to Disney for an audition. Her agent stood her ground but finally agreed to send Sharon out for a one-shot thing. Once there, she was offered the Mouseketeer job. The agent put up a valiant fight for a couple of weeks but then relented. Remembering Lonnie's belief that he was coerced into working for Disney, one has visions of heated telephone calls between the agent and the Disney casting department. But, of course, that's speculation.

Two weeks after she signed with Disney, that same agent called with the bad news that a major studio wanted to make a film called *The Shirley Temple Story* and had decided that there was only one kid in Hollywood who could play the lead: Sharon Baird. The Disney organization refused to relent so Sharon remained a Mouseketeer and the Shirley Temple movie went down the tubes.

Sharon is—I observe over tacos in a Mexican restaurant in New York at which she had requested we eat—a person of unshakable optimism and good cheer, so filled with manic conviviality and humor that, after an hour with her, one wants to begin screaming in a very loud voice: WAR, DEATH, PESTILENCE, SUICIDE, MURDER, RAPE, TORTURE. But, of course, one doesn't.

"I loved Walt Disney," Sharon says. "We had a lot of contact with him. I remember the first day when we were playing around the set, loudly, like kids do, when we looked up and there was Mr. Disney, in khakis, covered with paint from head to foot. He had been in the paint shop working with the designers. He was involved in everything.

"All the things he did came from the heart. He really cared about entertainment and people. You know, he had an apartment over the firehouse on Main Street out in Disneyland and he used to go there and stand by the window and watch the happy people come in and he'd just stand there with a big beam on his face."

Sharon was a standout Mouseketeer, of course, mainly because of her fantastic dancing and because she was teamed with Bobby, the tallest boy. She is remembered best for her jitterbug routines and a thing she and Bobby used to do which was called the wraparound and is just what it says.

Like Annette, her good friend, Sharon could barely wait to get to the studio in the morning. Those were such busy, happy days with lots of adults buzzing around, making over you, things like that. When the Mouse Club wasn't in production, Disney would send them on tour, or over to Disneyland to sign autographs. Like most of show business, it was hard work and when you fell into bed at night you were really tired but content. You knew that you had done your part to make a better world for the future. You really knew that.

After the Mouse Club, Sharon's career tapered off. Too old for child roles, too short for adult parts, Sharon returned to school. She occasionally made Vegas appearances with Donald O'Connor and made the Mouseketeer tours to Australia. After high school, she attended Valley College for two and a half years, majoring in math and secretarial science.

In 1964, she married Lee Thomas, a singer, and together with another male partner, they formed a group called Two Cats and a Mouse. They never made the Ed Sullivan Show but they did play a lot of clubs on the California-Nevada circuit. In 1969, she and Thomas split.

"He's still around here," Sharon says. "He lives not far from me. He owns a beauty shop. As a matter of fact, he cuts my hair. We're still good friends."

"I don't understand these here Hollywood arrangements," I say.

Sharon laughs. "It's not a Hollywood arrangement. It's a big world. There's room enough for both of us in it."

Somewhere, back in the early sixties, Sharon worked for a time as a secretary at Litton Industries. She didn't give up on show business, entirely. She would get odd jobs now and then, and when that ran out, fill in by working for Brown's Best in the West, a temporary office worker service. Finally, she took a steady job as a secretary for Blue Cross, a position which lasted three and a half years.

It looked, she admits, as though her show business career was finished.

"Then," Sharon says, "I got a call from Marty Krofft who was looking for short people for the 'Lidsville' show. I thought, sure, sure because I was pretty discouraged. But I went in and he gave me a job on the spot. It's been really good because I've gotten to do other things now . . . like I've been working with Raquel in

Vegas and around. Last year was the first year in a long time that I haven't had to work as a secretary."

"What do you do with Raquel?" I say.

"Oh, different things. I did a bend-over puppet. . . ."

"A what?"

"A bend-over puppet. Like, I bend over and there are two big dolls on my back. My arms are the legs of one of the dolls and my legs are the legs of the other one. Then I dance around and the dolls seem to be dancing together."

"Oh."

"And, another time I did a rock-and-roll wig which was this giant wig which was nothing but hair from head to foot."

Sharon and I walk back across town to the Statler-Hilton, the hotel where she is staying on this occasion, her first visit to New York. I point out the Empire State Building. Sharon smiles agreeably. We walk into the Statler's vast, unfriendly lobby, which has no furniture.

"What do you want to do, eventually?"

"I don't know," Sharon says. "I know I don't want to be a star. I guess I want to be an entertainer, a performer. Really, I guess, I just want to be able to dance."

Still, I can't help wondering what would have happened if Sharon had gotten to play the Shirley Temple lead. I've seen movies in which she did dance numbers with Martin and Lewis and Mitzi Gaynor. She was terrific. The kid could have been a contender.

I remembered that, earlier, Sharon had said one of the things that bothered her about being small was that people were always picking her up. She didn't mind, she said, if they asked first.

"Sharon," I say. "I'm going to pick you up now. Okay?"

"Okay," she says, with a giggle.

I pick her up. She is very light.

14

Roy

During the late 1930s and early 1940s—the golden age of animation when all of the most talented illustrators and artists in the business worked for Walt Disney—Roy Williams was a legend around the Disney studio.

Williams, a giant oak of a man with a brilliant mind for visual gags and a healthy imagination for developing stories of personal adventure, was admired by most of the other illustrators because of his incredible strength and for the stories he told. To this day, people swear they have seen Roy Williams lift cars, buses, all sorts of things. His adventures as a driver in those wild, prefreeway days were told, retold, embellished, to the point where they defy the imagination. Roy never bothered to deny them, though.

Williams, who was born in Coleville, Washington, but moved to Los Angeles at an early age, joined the Disney organization in 1929. He had majored in art, been the school cartoonist at Fremont High School, and been an outstanding football player. He wanted to draw, loved to draw, and was a competent draughtsman. His major talent, although he probably didn't realize it at the time, was in writing gags. Williams could take a situation and make it funny. He also loved, admired, worshiped, and was totally dedicated to Walt Disney.

"I started out with Walt," Williams says, in a gruff, difficult-to-follow baritone. "He took care of me for life."

Disney was fond of Williams also and he took him on. In a rare (for Disney) display of generosity, he even paid for Roy's training at the Chouinard Art School in Los Angeles for three years.

Williams became an important source of material for many of the Disney cartoon features. He did his job in a cheerful, un-complaining way, and if Walt had asked him to take a swan dive off the Empire State Building because he needed a shot of a fat man falling through space, Williams probably would have done that too.

Sharon Baird drives me over to Roy's house which is in Bur-bank only a few blocks from the studio he loves. His wife, Ethel, opens the door with a friendly flourish and we are inside. Roy is obviously delighted to see Sharon, lifting her up into his giant arms, as easily as if she were a teddy bear.

"I haven't seen you in months," he says, a hint of scold in his voice. "I love this little girl," he adds, turning to greet me. Sharon and Ethel go off to make some coffee and Roy invites me to see his pool.

Roy's pool. How to describe it, exactly, this friendly, kidney-shaped expanse of California blue where all the Mouseketeers used to come to swim, where Karen had her ninth birthday party. Roy's pool, and the environment he's built around it, looks like the set of a "Jungle Jim" movie. Grass-roofed huts line one side. Lava rocks sit on the other. For a time, Roy had the whole thing wired up so he could simulate a volcano. It's all very jungle landish. Roy built this incredible set for his daughter, Maureen, who is now married to millionaire Park Richardson and herself the mother of a fourteen-year-old daughter. On a tree, Roy has put the name "Lake Maureen" in carved wooden letters. The "u" has fallen off now, though, and he hasn't bothered to replace it.

Sitting there, watching the sunlight glint off Lake Maureen, Roy rambles on, in a friendly, glad-to-have-company sort of way. I asked Roy about the stories I had heard about his wild, impetuous youth.

"Don't put any of that stuff in," he says. "You know how things get exaggerated over the years. Most of that stuff was never true to begin with. When you get as old as I am you want to forget most of the stuff you've done.

"Life is a very strange thing, you know. Remember Bob Amsbery who was on the 'Mickey Mouse Club?' He used to ride to work with me every morning. He was always getting upset because I didn't watch the road when I drove. Then, he got killed in a car wreck. It's just odd. You can't ever tell. That's the mystery of life. You see handsome guys with big muscles and one day they just keel over and some of us fat and ugly guys go on forever. It's just part of the mystery of life."

"How did you happen to perform on the 'Mickey Mouse Club,'" I asked. "Had you ever acted before?"

"Oh, no," Roy says. "That just shows you again the genius of Walt Disney. Walt knew I loved kids and people even before I knew it. That's why he put me on a kids show. I'm a down-to-earth guy but I never dreamed of the kind of pleasure that working with those kids brought me. Walt knew. I didn't. That's why he was Walt Disney.

"One day he just called me in and said 'Say, you're funny-looking. I'm going to put you on the show and call you the Big Mouseketeer.' I said, 'Walt, I can't sing or dance or anything.' He said not to worry about it, I'd be good. Up till then, I had been working on the first story boards for the show and I designed the ears.

"No, I wasn't any actor. I could draw and do quick sketches. That was my main thing. I really didn't have to do much. I said my lines so badly that sometimes they'd wind up taking two words out of each take and putting them together. I did sing once but Walt heard it and threatened to fire everybody if they ever let me sing again. So, whenever we sang, I just mouthed the words."

Roy laughs, a solid, hearty laugh.

"Did you like Jimmie Dodd?"

"Everybody in the world liked Jimmie," Roy says. "He was a very religious man. He was an awfully sweet guy, full of love and kindness and patience. He was trying to convert me all the time. I used to say that Jimmie got all the angels and I got all the little rascals. Between us, we covered every kid in the world. . . . Have you met Ruth? She married a fine Christian man. They're fine people. I mean, I love God as much as anybody but I don't think you have to go to a building with a point on it to get to him. But they're fine people."

There is a hint of healthy agnosticism here. In a sense Roy played W. C. Fields to Jimmie's Jeanette MacDonald. But they were friends and there was a curious and strong bond between them.

I asked Roy if he had read the interview in *Rolling Stone* in which Dennis Day, one of the blue team Mouseketeers, had confessed to an appreciation of drugs and bisexuality and had made some unfavorable comments about his years with Disney.

"I think he showed poor judgment," Roy says. "I really don't know how he could do that. Dennis was an awfully sweet kid . . . he's still a sweet kid in spite of it. He had a very fine mother. I just don't know. . . . Maybe he did it in a weak moment or something."

"Tell me about some of the other kids?"

"They were all terrific—little Karen, and Sharon in there, I'm crazy about her. And Cheryl was so unspoiled. I remember when she married Lance Reventlow and they came over here for dinner one night. He was just a terrific, down-to-earth guy, just like you and me. Somebody spilled some peas and I picked one up in my fingers and said 'Anybody for marbles?' We all laughed and laughed. He was such a sweet guy. It's too bad. . . ."

Ethel brings some coffee and sets it down. She looks at Roy, who has had some ill health in recent years, most protectively.

"I'll tell you what I don't understand," Roy says, sipping his coffee. "I don't understand why Darlene never became a great singer. She was so talented but she just didn't have Annette's beauty and sex, you might say. I don't know . . . things happen to people. There's a thin line between success and failure. You just can't put your finger on it."

Roy rambles on but I am curious about some of the technical sides of the show. Why, for example, wasn't it done in color?

"I think it was because Walt felt that if something was good it would still be good no matter whether it was color or black and white. I doubt that money was the reason. Walt was . . . here's a great quote. Write this down. Walt always said 'You don't play over anybody's head or underneath them.'"

"What about—"

"Isn't that a great quote?"

"—the idea that the show really represented the spirit of Jimmie Dodd?"

"I mean, there were several people involved in the show but don't forget that the Big Brain—Walt—watched over everything."

I look at Roy closely to see if I can spot any look or inflection which might communicate irony, doubt, or bitterness, but it just isn't there.

His dedication to the Disney ideals is complete.

Consider this from Roy's biography, written by the Disney publicity people:

"Roy's art work and designs have appeared in *Life*, and *The New Yorker*. As a hobby, Roy drew for *The New Yorker*, resulting in the publication of several cartoon books.

"Through it all, Roy never forgot that *he owed it all to Walt Disney*. (My italics.) His feelings are best expressed in the dedication of one of his books.

"TO THE MAN WHO HAS MEANT THE MOST TO ME IN FAITH AND INSPIRATION, WALT DISNEY, WHOSE PATIENCE AND GUIDANCE THROUGH A LIFETIME OF ASSOCIATION ARE, IN THE GREATEST DEGREE IMAGINABLE, RESPONSIBLE FOR THE BEST OF ROY WILLIAMS."

So, there it is. How does one explain such devotion? Walt Disney never had a cartoon published in *The New Yorker*. And he never dedicated a book to Roy Williams, either. And, you want to know something, he didn't like kids all that much, either.

Roy had a book of cartoons called *How's the Back View Com-*

ing Along? published by Dutton in 1949 and another called *The Secret World of Roy Williams* published by Bantam Books in 1957. In 1967, Roy published a little book of poems about death with the Weather Bird Press. It is called *Vaporisms*.

He is also the man who invented the Mouse ears.

"They've sold millions of those things," Roy says. "I didn't get a royalty or anything. . . . Oh, when I left the studio I did get a nice little check. Instead of giving me a party, they gave me a check. That was much nicer. Don't put that in, though. Maybe, some people didn't get a check."

I didn't say I wouldn't.

"My whole life with Disney has been one big laugh," Roy says. "I've had nothing but fun. I have no complaints."

"Wouldn't you say that the spirit of the 'Mickey Mouse Club' belonged primarily to Jimmie Dodd, though?"

"It was Jimmie's spirit," Roy says, "but don't forget that behind it all was Walt Disney who came in and made changes and put the magic touch on it."

I am going over to the Disney studio and Roy insists on driving me there. I suspect he just wants an excuse to go there.

We move down South Buena Vista toward the studio in Roy's big van. These days, at least, he is a good and cautious driver.

Roy tells me about a cemetery plot he has bought at Forest Lawn. He tells me about a society that one joins that will bury you for only fifty dollars but they don't tell anyone what they do with the bodies. He mentions Ward Kimball, the great animator, known in some circles as Disney's artistic conscience.

I nod at the appropriate moments but I am thinking about Walt Disney. If the man had a talent, I thought, it was in inspiring fantastic loyalty in people who were better than the projects he most often asked them to work on. Better, too, than his own ability to reciprocate their devotion.

The men who put the "Mickey Mouse Club" together, for example—Bill Walsh, Jimmie Dodd, Dick Darley, Hal Adelquist, Sid Miller, Roy—were above-average talents and they succeeded in making a show that was better than it should have been, considering Disney's personal disdain for the project.

Walt Disney had some sort of genius for attracting people of genuine talent who often did things of genius which caused some people to conclude that Disney, himself, was a genius. Some of them, like Ward Kimball, Ub Iwerks, and Walsh, really were, and they made Disney seem so.

The question, of course, is just how long can the Disney organization continue to attract men of this caliber without the Big Brain himself? Disney Productions today is run by bookkeepers whose idea of creativity is to send a flunky over to NBC to study "Laugh-In" and come up with an abomination like the "Mouse Factory" which is an insult to the viewer and to the good things Disney has done.

There will never be another "Mickey Mouse Club" like the original simply because the creative impetus is not there. Disney today is monetarily rich and creatively bankrupt and eventually this bankruptcy will catch up with it. Shed no tears. When the show ended production, several of the kids asked to keep their ears. Disney refused to let them do so.

A kid with a bicycle stands on an island in the middle of the street. Roy stops and waves him across.

The kid waves back and refuses to move. Roy waves again. The kid waves again. Stalemate.

Finally, after what seems to be an interminable length of time, Roy drives on.

"I don't know," he says, more than a little sadness in his voice. "Somehow, they just aren't like they used to be. These kids now are different. Don't you think so?"

15

Annette —
The Everyday Housewife
and the End

An ordinary afternoon in Encino.

"What time is it?" Annette says, glancing absently at her watchless wrist. "Gina should have been home by now."

Gina is Annette's seven-year-old daughter and she is late from school.

"Maybe she stopped at a friend's house," offers Sharon Baird, who is visiting this particular day. Sharon and Annette have remained friendly over the years since the Mouse Club and occasionally get together.

"Maybe," Annette says. She looks unconvinced.

We are gathered in a comfortable little sitting room at Annette's house. Annette, Sharon, an affectionate cockapoo dog named Daisy Clover, and me. Through the spacious windows in back, the afternoon sun glints harshly off the cerulean blue pool. The house itself is a big, rambling ranch-style number sited on a corner lot and decorated in a kind of tasteful Angelo's of Mulberry Street manner with lots of glass and mirrors and modern renaissance details. It is not what one usually thinks of as a movie star's home with pillars and staircases and dramatic details. It is a nice house but not a great one, and it reads more successful-middle-management executive than rich. The phone rings and Annette goes to answer.

"No, they haven't come yet. . . ."

"Annette made these herself," Sharon says, pointing to a needlepoint cushion with the word LOVE spelled out on it and to a framed needlepoint of W. C. Fields pouring himself a drink with the word DRAT on it. Next to W.C. is a Charlie Shultz cartoon which shows Charlie Brown saying: "I can't believe it. . . . Annette Funicello is 30."

"I'll have her call the minute she gets here. . . . Okay . . . bye."

Annette walks back to her chair. She has a confident walk and she is extremely well put together.

"I went back to Disney to do a Mouse Factory show (a syndicated program the studio has been doing the past several years) recently," Annette says. "It was really great to see the crew and the electricians and the people we worked with on the Mouse Club."

"Was Jack Whitman, Jr., still there?" Sharon says, a mischievous look in her eye.

"No, he's doing 'Hawaii Five-O,'" Annette says, turning to me. "That was my big love. My big, big love. His father was a camera operator and Jack was a clanker. . . . You know, the guy that hits the thing and yells TAKE ONE. Jack the Clanker, we called him."

Sharon and Annette giggle.

"What ever happened to your T-Bird?" Sharon asks.

"I gave that to my brother Mike a couple of years ago when I got my XKE," Annette says. "My parents gave me this T-Bird for my sixteenth birthday. It was white when I got it but I had it specialized . . . forty coats of paint and it came out purple. My father says he knew it was the car for me when he saw it on the lot. The license plate was MMC—Mickey Mouse Club. Isn't that— hey, big boy, where did you come from?"

It is Annette's four-year-old, Jack Gilardi, Jr., waking up from a nap.

"Are you hungry?" Annette says. "Do you want a sandwich?" Jackie shakes his head no.

"Do you have to potty?" Again, no.

"Well, go get your vest and Mommy will put it on."

Jackie shuffles off to get his vest.

"I love rough-and-tumble little boys," Annette says. "I have a feeling I'm due for twins next, though. I have the names all picked out . . . Joey and Jolene Gilardi. Doesn't that have a nice ring?"

"That's good," Sharon says.

"That's the thing about doing films," Annette says, answering a question I haven't asked. "I'd like to do a good serious part but I'd have to leave the children at my parents' house. I wouldn't get to see them. The reason I got married is to have children. They're my responsibility, not my parents'. I just don't want to do that. My last picture was *Thunder Alley* with Frankie Avalon and Fabian in 1968. I just don't want to get involved in a tight shooting schedule."

She pauses to light a cigarette.

"My husband, being my agent, brings home scripts all the time. I read about ten pages of them and it just becomes ridiculous. By page ten, I've been raped or I'm smoking pot. We both just sit there and laugh. They're just not for me. . . . Jackie, get a Kleenex. Look at your nose."

Just now, Gina and her friend come in.

"Where have you been?" Annette says. "Caroline, call your mother immediately. She's very worried."

Annette wipes Jackie's nose with a tissue and buttons up his vest.

"Would you like a cookie?" she asks.

He shakes his head no.

"Would you like chocolate milk?"

"No."

"Would you like a punch in the nose?"

Jackie laughs. He loves it.

"I don't know," Annette says. "I guess I just got very spoiled working for Mr. Disney. My every move was watched. They treated me just like my parents did at home. I really liked working. My mother tells me I would be up before the alarm went off at five. It was just super. We had some great times."

"Remember that party at Margene Storey's?" Sharon says.

"Sure," Annette says, giggling. "We all jumped into the pool and all the neighbors were scandalized. They all said 'those horrible Mouseketeers.' We all had our clothes on, though, and it was really nothing."

"How about the hay ride?"

"Oh yeah," she says. "My parents were still living in Studio City then. Poor Shelley. I'll never forget. Shelley Fabares didn't have a date so she sat up front and talked to the driver."

"Do your parents live nearby?"

"Three minutes away," Annette says. "I see them about every day. Jackie's big kick is to go down to the garage and ride the lift with his grandfather."

Gina and her friend come back into the room.

"Mommy, I don't want Jackie to play," Gina says. "He's all messy." Jackie has changed his mind about the cookies and there is telltale chocolate all over his face. Annette wipes it off.

"Did you bring a picture?" he asks Sharon. "Gina wants a picture of you from the show." Annette explains to Caroline that Sharon is one of the stars of "Lidsville" and "H. R. Pufnstuf." Sharon produces a photo and Annette asks her to autograph it for Gina. Annette's fuss over Sharon's rather minor role on the show is just a bit too emphatic, a hint too kind, but is done without a trace of condescension.

"Have you ever thought of doing something other than pictures? Nightclubs, maybe?"

"People ask me that all the time," Annette says. "They all

A Meeting of Mice. Front row: Mary, Tommy, Sharon, and Sherry. Back row: Eileen (with her new arrival), Judy, Lynn, Bonni, Billie Jean, Margene, and Karen.

From left: Billie Jean Beanblossom, Tommy, Sherry, and Bonni Kern. Billie Jean worked as a professional dancer and teacher before marrying Ted Cooper, a senior buyer at Lockheed. The mother of two, she now works as a personal secretary at Valley-Todeco, Inc. Bonni has been an executive in several businesses. She is married to Harold "Bud" Carr, a driver for United Parcel Service. They have two children and live in Alhambra, California.

Mary Sartori attended Pasadena City College, was in a movie called Sheriff of Cochise, and is now married to Lee Celano, a wholesale meat dealer. They have two boys and live in Glendale, California. (above left)

Margene Storey went to beauty college and spent six years as a hair stylist. She now sells automobiles. She is divorced and has two children. (above right)

Judy Harriet did television and nightclub work before marrying Tony Richmond. They have two daughters. (below left)

Eileen Diamond was in several stage musicals before marrying Roy Rogosin, a composer-conductor. She and her husband are working on a stage version of The Umbrellas of Cherbourg. They have two children and live in North Hollywood. (below right)

Dickie Dodd has been an actor and rock musician. He was once in a group called The Standells, which had a couple of hits. (above left)

Tommy Cole and Bonnie Lynn Fields strike a Hollywood pose. Tommy worked as a makeup man for NBC in Burbank before setting out on his own last year. Bonnie went to business college, danced in films like Sweet Charity, Bye Bye Birdie, and Funny Girl, and is now business manager of Century Leasing & Management Company in Los Angeles. She is single. (above right)

Mary Espinosa was known to the other kids as "upside-down Mary" because of her acrobatic ability. She now works for the Family Health Program in Long Beach, has a son and daughter, and is recently divorced. (below left)

The couple today. Karen Pendleton worked for Prudential, is married to a lawyer, and has a daughter. Cubby O'Brien now plays drums for The Carpenters, among other things. Cubby's wife, Marilyn, is a singer. (below right)

On January 17–18, 1976, the Disney publicity department sponsored a Mouseketeer reunion at Disneyland. Considering that there would be no pay, attendance was good—although Lonnie Burr canceled when the Disney folks balked at paying $11.25 in car fare. All the reunion pictures were taken by Gene Daniels of Black Star.

Roy Williams, the Big Mooseketeer, draws a picture of Mickey for a young fan.

want to write material for me. I come out and whip off the ears and the T-shirt. I think it would be terrific. But, after I take the costume off, then what do I do for an hour?"

Annette smiles, a sweet, innocent killer of a smile and my heart does that funny little number it used to do when I was twelve years old and she was a little black-and-white figure in strange ears living in a snowy twenty-one-inch landscape.

"No," she says, almost sadly I think but I could be mistaken. "I'm just not interested in that. My life is very full with the children. It's okay for some people but it's just not right for me."

You can tell that she means it, too.

APPENDIX

The "Mickey Mouse Club" was seen daily, Monday through Friday, on ABC between 5 P.M. and 6 P.M. It was divided into four regular segments:

(1) NEWSREEL, JIMINY CRICKET, or SOOTY—Filmed on location around the world, the NEWSREELS were considered by many the most "educational" aspect of the show. JIMINY CRICKET, created largely by Disney's ace animator Ward Kimball for the 1939 film *Pinocchio*, starred in a series on safety and common sense called "I'm No Fool." SOOTY was a hand puppet discovered in England by Disney's then merchandising director O. B. Johnston. It never caught on and most viewers have trouble remembering SOOTY at all.

(2) MOUSEKETEERS—The Mouseketeer segment was divided into five different formats:
     1. Monday—"Fun With Music Day"
     2. Tuesday—"Guest Star Day"
     3. Wednesday—"Anything Can Happen Day"
     4. Thursday—"Circus Day"
     5. Friday—"Talent Round-Up Day"
The "red" team—those Mouseketeers who appeared in the Roll Call—appeared in the segment on Monday, Wednesday, and Friday. The "blue" team appeared Tuesday and Thursday.

(3) SERIALS—During the 1955–56 season, the serials were:
     1. TWA serial "What I Want to Be."
     2. "Spin & Marty."   24 episodes.
     3. "Corky and White Shadow."   17 episodes.

4. "Border Collie."   4 episodes.
5. "Let's Go."   5 episodes.
6. "Foreign Correspondent."   5 episodes.
7. "Christmas Around the World."   5 episodes.
8. "Animal Autobiographies."   5 episodes.

(4) CARTOON—The heart of the show was the Disney backlog of cartoons. Over 100 different films were used during the season.

1956–1957

The segments remained the same with the exception of the serials and the addition of Doddisms, which alternated with the cartoons.

The 1956–57 SERIALS were:
1. "Hardy Boys."   20 episodes.
2. "Animal Autobiographies": *Camel, Baboon, Bee, Elephant, Alaskan Sled Dog.*
3. "Adventure in Dairyland."   8 segments.
4. "The Further Adventures of Spin & Marty."
5. "Christmas Around the World": *Germany, Canada, Japan, England, Denmark.*
6. "First Americans": *Origin of the Indians, Indians on Horseback, Indians of Yesterday, Indians of Today.*
7. "Sierra Pack Trip."   5 episodes.
8. "Secret of Mystery Lake Film Serial."   7 episodes.
9. *Eagle Hunters.*
10. "Children of the World": *Arctic, Samoa, Siam.*
11. "Mouseketeer to Samoa."   5 episodes.
12. "Boys of the Western Sea."   8 segments.
13. "Junior Safari."   5 episodes.

1957–1958

Half-hour shows:

(1) MICKEY MOUSE CLUB MARCH

(2) MOUSEKETEERS:
1. "Mouseketeers."

2. "Mousekartoon."
3. "Mousekatour to England."
4. "Newsreel" (Doreen, Tommy Cole, Don Agrati).
5. "Talent Round-Up."
6. "Mouseka-preview."

(3) HARDY BOYS ("Ghost Farm"—15 segments. Sequel, first
    time used).
    NEWSREEL SPECIALS:
    1. "Hawaiian Adventure."
    2. "Encyclopedia—Uranium."
    3. "Argentine Adventure."
    4. "Tommy Cole Series": 10 Newsgathering; 4 Miscellaneous.
    5. David Stollery: "Youth Takes Over the Atom."
    6. "Geisha."

(4) SERIALS:
    1. "Spin & Marty," 2nd sequel.
    2. "Clint and MacFilm Serial." 15 episodes.
    3. "Annette Film Serial." 20 episodes.

1958–1959

This year, half-hour shows were re-edited from 1955–56 and 1956–57.

MONDAY, WEDNESDAY, and FRIDAY
    1. "Mickey Mouse March."
    2. "Fun with Music Day."
    3. "Guest Star Day."
    4. "Anything Can Happen Day."
    5. "Circus Day."
    6. "Talent Round-Up Day."
    7. "Mickey Mouse Tag."
    8. "Alma Mater of the Day."

CORRESPONDENTS: England, Japan, Denmark
    1. "Jiminy Cricket."
    2. "Christmas Around the World."
    3. "Donald Duck's Drawing Lesson."

  4. "Encyclopedia."
  5. "Sooty."
  6. "Newsreels."
  7. "Newsreel Specials."

TUESDAY and THURSDAY
  1. "Spin & Marty."
  2. "What I Want to Be."
  3. "Corky and White Shadow."
  4. "Scamp (Border Collie)."
  5. "Secret of Mystery Lake."
  6. "Skin Diving and Shark Hunting."
  7. "San Juan River Expedition."
  8. "The Hardy Boys."
  9. "Adventure in Dairyland."
  10. "Eagle Hunters."
  11. "Sierra Pack Trip."
  12. "Adventure in the Magic Kingdom."

Although its network run ended at the close of the 1959 season, the "Mickey Mouse Club" was seen in syndication between 1962 and 1965. Existing material was used as well as a few new features.

SERIALS

Among the most memorable aspects of the MMC were the daily serials. The following is a summary of the serials as described in studio press releases. The prose style is lacking but the ideas are there:

  (1) "WHAT I WANT TO BE."
      Airline hostess or pilot, filmed at Trans World Airlines headquarters in Kansas City, depicting special training procedures for becoming an airline stewardess and a pilot. Pat Morrow and Duncan Richardson were to get their wings and fly aboard TWA's Super Constellation.   10 episodes.

  (2) "CORRESPONDENTS":   5 episodes each
      England   (Dick Metzger)
      Japan   (George Nagata)
      Mexico   (Gabriel Lopez)
      Italy   (Annette Funicello)

(3) "LET'S GO SERIES": 5 episodes. "Let's Go" to:
Arizona School for Boys — (Photographers:
Skin Diving ———————— (Lloyd Mason Smith
Exploring with Kiko ——— (Lee Chaney
Shark Hunting ——————— (Tad Nichols
Elephant Round-up ——— (Doane Hoag, Lee Chaney,
Alvy Moore)

(4) "CHRISTMAS AROUND THE WORLD"
Switzerland
Holland
Mexico
Denmark
Sweden (I and II)

(5) "ANIMAL AUTOBIOGRAPHIES": Individual shows
Buffalo   *Giraffes*
Coyote   *Mountain Lion*
Black Bear   *Bee*
Prairie Dog   *Baboon*
King of Beasts

(6) "SAN JUAN RIVER EXPEDITION": 5 episodes

(7) "SIERRA PACK TRIP": 5 episodes. Produced by Bill
Walsh; Directed by William Beaudine; Narrated by Lee
Chaney.

(8) "CHILDREN OF THE WORLD":
Children of the Arctic. Directed and narrated by Charles
Shows. Photography by Alfred and Alma Milotte.
Children of Siam. Directed and narrated by Charles Shows.
Photographer, Herbert Knapp.
Junior Safari to Africa. Directed by Edward Sampson; Nar-
rated by Ray Darby; Produced by Bill Walsh; Photogra-
pher, Walter Castle.

(9) "Boys of the Western Sea": Bjorne Jensen; written by Astrid
Henning.

(10) "A Mouseketeer to Samoa": Produced by Bill Walsh. Narrated by Ray Darby.

(11) "Border Collie": Produced by Bill Walsh; directed by Larry Lansburgh; written by Bill Cox.

(12) *Alaskan Sled Dog*: Produced by Bill Walsh. Narrated by Charles Shows.

(13) NEWSREEL SPECIALS: Each program had many episodes.
   1. "Argentine Adventure"
   2. "Newsgathering"
   3. "Youth Takes Over the Atom"
   4. "Uranium Hunt"
   5. "Inside Report on Washington": *The Congress; The FBI; Money*
   6. "Geisha Girl"
   7. "Cormorant Fishing"
   8. "Lobster Trapping"

(14) "You, the Human Animal": Produced by Bill Walsh. Directed by Les Clark.

(15) "Spin & Marty": 1955–1956. 24 episodes.
   A series about a group of teen-age boys spending their summer on a western ranch. DAVID STOLLERY as Marty Markham, a city boy, and TIM CONSIDINE as Spin, a ranch boy, lead the cast. It is based on the book *Marty Markham* by Lawrence Edward Watkins, adapted and directed by William Beaudine.

   Marty, the city boy, antagonizes everyone by calling the TRIPLE R RANCH a dirty old ranch. He is afraid of horses, however, and is harassed by the others. Ready to return home, his family butler teaches him and holds him there. Later, in calf roping, he has to learn again.

   Produced by Bill Walsh; written by Lillie Hayward; directed by William Beaudine, Fred Hartsook; Teleplay by Jackson Gillis.

(16) "Further Adventures of Spin & Marty": 1956–1957

Spin Evans (TIM CONSIDINE) and Marty Markham (DAVID STOLLERY) and Moochie (KEVIN CORCO-RAN) all return to the Triple R Ranch for another summer together. Marty doesn't put on any airs; he's now one of the fellows and pitches right in to the work.

A girls' camp is on the other side of the lake, so the boys do a lot of practicing for the upcoming swimming meet with North Fork.

The girls are invited to a dance at the Triple R. Spin and Marty meet Annette (ANNETTE FUNICELLO) and Peggy (MELINDA PLOWMAN). Immediately, Marty has a crush on Annette.

When the girls are out riding, a runaway horse frightens them. Annette's horse runs off, but the boys save everyone.

The girls go to the Triple R for a social evening and Spin develops a crush on Annette. Now Spin and Marty begin to vie for the favors of Annette. The adults, Bill Burnett and Miss Adams are also attracted. Everyone is in a love-sick daze, broken only by Moochie, who plunges from the high dive and cannot swim, so everyone jumps in to rescue him.

Later on Spin is so jealous of Annette that he rides off in a rage and is thrown from his horse; when he is missing, the boys find him unconscious. Getting him back to the ranch, they call a doctor.

Moochie is supposed to care for the wonderful horse, Sky-rocket, who is in a lather; but in the excitement, the boy doesn't do it, and the horse contracts pneumonia. The vet can't save the horse, but at the last moment Ollie admin-isters an old-fashioned remedy, and the horse is saved. Moochie doesn't know and, filled with remorse, he runs away. With the recuperation of the horse and of Spin, the ranch returns to normal. Then Moochie is found and brought back.

The boys build a pavilion for the upcoming dance. Marty and Perkins get stung by bees while gathering greens to decorate the stage, and are confined to bed during the dance, when Grandma arrives again. Marty's sorrows are compounded by Annette's being with Spin having a wonderful time.

Just before the swimming meet, Spin and Marty have a fight in the corral which doesn't help the morale for the winning team. But when the meet is on, Moochie, Spin, and Marty win their events and Annette excitedly urges them on.

Spin accidentally swims into a boat and is knocked unconscious. Marty rescues him. Thus the two renew their friendship, but fickle Annette goes off with the champion of the North Fork Team. So, friends again, Spin and Marty vow to stay away from girls.

(17) "Corky and White Shadow": 1955–1956.   17 episodes and introductions.

Two robbers, Eddy and Durango Dude, hold up a bank in Glen Forks. Sheriff Matt Brady (BUDDY EBSEN) goes after them; Eddy is shot and captured, but Durango Dude is shot and escapes. A posse tracks them, and Corky (DARLENE GILLESPIE) takes her dog WHITE SHADOW into the woods looking for him. She visits her Uncle Dan at his cabin. They find a wounded man, not knowing it is Dude. They send White Shadow for Matt who comes, but he threatens Corky's life, so Sheriff loses his man.

Corky goes back into the woods and this time Dude ties her to a tree and a snake comes at her. Dude fires his gun to kill the snake. The gunfire betrays his hiding place and he is captured.

Meanwhile, Eddy escapes from jail and then frees Dude. They go to Dan's cabin, hold him as hostage. Corky and Freddie have gone into the woods again looking for White Shadow who has vanished. They find the crooks, alert Sheriff who is in the woods, and the robbers are finally captured together. White Shadow turns up in a canyon nearby with a female coyote, considered an unusual combination.

(18) "The Dairy Story":   8 segments—open, close. Walt Disney sends Annette Funicello and Sammy Ogg on a two week visit to the 560-acre Sugar River Farm or Sisk Dairy Farm ten miles from Madison, Wisconsin. Mr. and Mrs. Mc-Candless and their three children show the Mouseketeers how their big dairy farm is run. They explore the stanchion barn and the loafing barn; the milking machines and the processing of the milk. They ride on tractors, hay wagons, watch crop dusting and, then, mowing of the fields. Corn, oats, and hay grown on the farm make it self-sustaining.

The dairy herd is a 1975 head of prize Holsteins producing 2,000 pounds of milk each day. The big Holstein bull, Romeo, weighs a ton and is awesome. On the last day of the visit the operation of the farm is left to Annette and Sammy while the McCandless family goes off. But an electrical storm throws out the milking equipment and one of the cows throws her calf. The young stars call back the farm family and everything ends up happily.

For fun, a 4-H dance is held. The Swiss handyman who does everything from rescuing children to Swiss yodeling fills in with comedy. The children in the family are made honorary Mouseketeers and they watch the Mickey Mouse show about their own farm back home on television.

Produced by Bill Walsh, from a screenplay by Lillie Hayward. Directed by Bill Beaudine.

(19) "The Secret of Mystery Lake": 7 parts. 1956–1957
The adventures of a young naturalist, Bill Richards (GEORGE FENNEMAN), who attempts to photograph the wild rare beauty of the animals, birds, and exotic wild-life of the swamp. Some animals he cages to study and film further, but finds them all released. He learns the culprit is a young blond woman, Laney Thorne (GLORIA MAR-SHALL). When she understands he is a naturalist and will not harm the creatures she co-operates. He needs to locate and film a rare and valuable egret colony living on an island in the Moccasin Swamp which is owned by an old and dangerous hermit, Bill Bogue, who won't allow anyone near his

birds. At risk to their lives, the new-found friends invade the area; but the hermit catches them, smashes their oars and drives them waist deep through the snake-ridden swamp to safety. But Bill has gained a lot of knowledge and happiness, and the love of a girl, so we are not sure whether he leaves there or not.

> Directed by Larry Lansburgh. Screenplay by John and Rosalie Bodrero from original story by Janet Lansburgh. Actors: George Fenneman and Gloria Marshall.

(20) "The Hardy Boys": 1956–1957

Frank and Joe Hardy are the sons of a detective. They have a mystery in their own neighborhood which is a report of a lost pirate treasure supposed to be hidden at nearby Applegate mansion. The boys are looking for it, and Iola, Joe's girlfriend, is helping them. Fenton Hardy, the father, is away on another case and the boys' Aunt Gertrude is looking after them.

Perry Robinson, a young boy fugitive, is working at the estate, and the plumber, Jackley, finds a lot of tools in the boy's room. Perry gives Joe a gold doubloon and they let him hide out, but eventually the juvenile authorities show up and he is taken away.

Frank and Joe meet Applegate who explains to the boys that the treasure is a reality, and it was given by LaFitte to Applegate's grandfather in repayment for the burning of the Applegate plantation many years before.

A mysterious stranger appears on the scene. Jackley is knocked out, and Iola is terribly frightened. Fenton Hardy returns and goes immediately to the estate where Iola tells him the stranger is upstairs. It is a man named Boles and he is captured and questioned. The two boys go to Boles's room in town, and they find a gold doubloon hidden in his shoe which has a torn message in it. The message tells there is a treasure somewhere there, and the man who wrote it, a Jenkins, is in prison.

Then it turns out that Jackley, the plumber, was once in prison also, and was a cellmate of Jenkins! Boles is released from prison since the treasure is not found. Jackley comes to Boles and asks him to be his new partner. Under duress, Boles accepts. He sends Jackley outside to watch for the boys, and then phones the police to pick him up. Jackley spots the two boys and follows them to a water tower which they think is the tower where the treasure is hidden. Frank falls through a floor and discovers the treasure. He yells, which draws Jackley.

The boys are terrified to learn Jackley and Boles are partners in crime. Meanwhile, police and Boles converge—the criminals are knocked out and carried off to prison.

The treasure is unearthed. In her relief and happiness, Iola kisses Frank.

> Directed by Charles Haas. Teleplay by Jackson Gillis based on *The Tower Treasure* by Frank W. Dixon.

(21) "The Hardy Boys #2": 1957–1958. "The Mystery of Ghost Farm." 15 episodes.

(From press releases.) In this second Hardy Boys serial the youths try to solve the mystery of a haunted farm. These further adventures are titled "The Mystery of Ghost Farm" and concern a farmer who died, leaving no one to care for his animals. Plans are made to destroy the livestock, but the Hardy boys step in to prevent this. They are assisted in their efforts by a mysterious ghost and uncover a clever scheme on the part of a relative of the farmer to claim a false inheritance. The boys are older in this serial, and though Joe is still annoyed by the attentions of winsome young Iola Morton, Frank has reached the stage where he suffers strange lapses at the sight of a pretty girl.

(22) "Clint and Mac": 1957–1958. 15 episodes.

"Clint and Mac" tells of an American boy, Clint, son of a U.S. Air Force officer stationed in London, and an English boy, Mac, son of a Scotland Yard inspector. The two boys innocently become involved with a band of criminals who have stolen the original manuscript of *Treasure Island* from the British Museum. When the crooks try to smuggle the manuscript out of England, the two boys trail them across London to the river. The climax is reached in an exciting chase down the Thames, with the boys bringing about the capture of the thieves and the restoration of the manuscript.

Neil Wolfe, sixteen, son of an American Air Force colonel formerly stationed in England, portrays the role of Clint. Jonathan Bailey, thirteen-year-old English actor, plays Mac. Portraying the role of Pamela is thirteen-year-old English actress Sandra Michaels. (From press releases.)

(23) "Annette" 1957–1958. 15 episodes. (By some strange quirk, Disney press releases at the time of this writing list the title of this show as "Annette and Darlene." Darlene wasn't in it. The show starred Annette, Tim Considine, and Roberta Shore. Mouseketeers Sharon and Doreen had supporting roles.) Annette is the story of a teen-age girl who has been raised simply; a country girl who suddenly finds herself living with city relatives and must cope with the more formal patterns of city life. It is based on the book, *Margaret*, by Janette Sebring Lowrey. It is the story of a young teen-ager in a small city—of her struggle to gain poise and confidence in herself, even against jealousies, and her ultimate successful overcoming of life's challenges.

One of the most memorable incidents of this series is a missing necklace that Laura (played by Roberta Shore) believes Annette, a new girl in town, has stolen. The necklace is later found in the piano. Laura apologizes to Annette and sings a wonderful song called "Don't Jump to Conclusions."

(24) "Spin & Marty #3": 1957–1958. 29 episodes.
The third season at the Triple R Ranch gets off to an explosive start as Spin (TIM CONSIDINE) and Marty (DAVID STOLLERY) arrive together, riding in an old jalopy they have made during the winter. As the two resume their friendships with their pals, activities at the ranch move quickly. Moochie (KEVIN CORCORAN) wins his pleas to keep two small white rabbits against the better judgment of the counselor, Bill Burnett (HARRY CAREY, JR.).

Dynamite, the wild white stallion, causes trouble. But the biggest tragedy is caused by Speckle who crashes Marty's car into the kitchen, causing much damage.

But it is this very expensive mishap that brings the new serial to a musical climax. With the aid of Darlene, one of the girls from an adjoining summer camp, the youngsters put on a musical show to earn enough money to pay for the kitchen repairs. Meanwhile, there is youthful romancing among Spin, Marty, Darlene, and Annette, but as the summer comes to an end, the boys and girls are left happily planning for another summer vacation.

"MICKEY MOUSE CLUB" TV CREDITS   1955 through 1959

PRODUCER
Bill Walsh

ASSOCIATE PRODUCER
Mike Holoboff
Louis Debney
Tommy Walker
Malcolm Stuart Boylan

GENERAL CO-ORDINATOR
Mike Holoboff
Hal Adelquist
Chuck Dargan

DIRECTORS

Sidney Miller	Edward Sampson
Dik Darley	Charles Barton
Jonathan Beaudine, Jr.	Fred Hartsook
William Beaudine, Jr.	Montie Montana
Charles Haas	Charles Lamont
Larry Lansburgh	Hamilton S. Luske
Charles Shows	Clyde Geronimi
Robert G. Shannon	Tommy Walker
R. G. Springsteen	

ASSISTANT DIRECTORS

Jack Cunningham
William Beaudine, Jr.
Dolph Zimmer
Russ Haverick
Horace Hough
Erich von Stroheim, Jr.
Vincent McEveety

Joseph L. McEveety
Tommy Foulkes
Les Gorall
Bill Finnegan
Les Philmer
Art Vitarelli
Gene Law

CAMERAMEN (Directors of Photography)

Gordon Avil, ASC
Edward Coleman, ASC
Walter H. Castel, ASC
John Martin
W. W. Goodpaster
Karl Maslowski
Herbert Knapp
Frederick Gately

Al Runkie
Doane R. Hoag
Lloyd Mason Smith
Tad Nichols
J. Carlos Carbajal
Charles P. Boyle, ASC
Arthur J. Ornitz

FILM EDITORS

Cotton Warburton, ACE
Al Teeter
Joseph S. Dietrick
George Nicholson
John O. Young
Lee Huntington
Robert Stafford
George Gale, ACE

Jack Vandagriff
Ed Sampson
Jim Love
Wayne Hughes
Laurie Vejar
Edward R. Baker
Lloyd Richardson
Hugh Chaloupka, Jr.
Ernest Palmer

Carlos Savage
Ellsworth Hoagland, ACE
Anthony Gerard
Stanley Johnson, ACE
Bill Lewis
Paul Capon

SPECIAL PROCESSES

Ub Iwerks, ASC
Eustace Lycett

MUSIC

Buddy Baker
Franklyn Marks
Joseph S. Dubin
William Lava
Joseph Mullendore
Paul Smith
Oliver Wallace

Herman D. Koppel
Clifford Vaughn
Frank Worth
Richard Aurandt
Jaime Mendoza Nava
Temple Abady
Edward Plumb

SONGS

Jimmie Dodd	Cliff Edwards	Sidney Fine
Gil George	Franklyn Marks	Ron Salt
Charlie Shows	Sam Sykens	Jeanne Gayle
Tom Adair	Bob Russell	Ed Penner
Larry Orenstein	Ray Darby	Mack David
Bob Amsberry	George Bruns	Al Hoffman
Ruth Carrell	Jack Spiers	Jerry Livingston
Stan Jones	Paul Smith	Marvin Ash
Larry Adelson	Muzzy Marceleno	Ray Brenne
Roy Williams	Erdman Penner	Carl Sigman
Martin Schwab	Larry Morey	Bob Jackman
Imogene Carpenter	Eliot Daniel	Fess Parker
Oliver Wallace	Frances Jeffords	Buddy Ebsen

CONDUCTOR
Leo Damiani (Burbank Symphony)
Because of the numerous credits on animated films, both originals created especially for the MMC, and those cartoons already in the film library of Walt Disney Productions, credits will be given on request only, upon identification of cartoon or program.

SOUND
Robert O. Cook
Sid A. Manor

RERECORDING
Reese Overacker

CHOREOGRAPHY
Tom Mahoney
Burch Holtzman (Burch Mann)

ART DIRECTORS
Bruce Bushman
Marvin Aubrey Davis
Carroll Clark

SET DECORATION
Bertram Granger
Fred MacLean

Emil Kuri
William L. Stevens
Vin Taylor
Armor E. Goetten

COSTUME
Chuck Keehne

MAKEUP
Pat McNalley
Tom Bartholomew
David Newell
Joe Hadley

FACILITIES CO-ORDINATOR
Ben Harris

PRODUCTION MANAGERS
Ben Chapman
Mike Holoboff
Douglas Pierce

PRODUCTION SUPERVISORS
Mike Holoboff
Lou Debney
Perce Pearce
Alan L. Jaggs
Stirling Silliphant
Bill Park
Hal Ramser
Charles Shows
Ben Sharpsteen
Harry Tytle
Jack Cutting
Gene Armstrong
Larry Clemens

RCA SOUND RECORDING

TECHNICAL FACILITIES
   Mark Amistead TV Inc.

WRITERS
   Lillie Hayward
   Lee Chaney
   Bill Cox
   Jackson Gillis
   Charles Shows
   John & Rosalie Bodrero
   Astrid Henning
   Charles Haas
   Larry Clemens
   Janet Lansburgh

PRODUCT DEVELOPMENT
The following list of subsidiary products developed out of the "Mickey
Mouse Club" is included not only for historic reasons but also to dem-
onstrate the incredible genius of the Disney organization in the field
of marketing. Nothing, as you will see, was forgotten.

RECORDINGS (Disneyland Record Company)

MM12   *The Musical Highlights from the Mickey Mouse Club* TV
           Show
MM14   *Twenty-seven New Songs from the Mickey Mouse Club* TV
           Show
MM18   *We're the Mouseketeers*
MM20   *Walt Disney's Song Fest*
DQ1229 *Songs from the Mickey Mouse Club Serials*
MM24   *Annette and Songs from Disney Serials*
MM32   *Sleeping Beauty by Darlene Gillespie*

For reasons not entirely clear to me, Disney press releases fail to
mention the following Mouseketeer records distributed by Am-Par
Record Corporation of Los Angeles:

DBR-75   *Karen and Cubby*
DBR-74   *Mickey's Big Show*
DBR-71   *We're the Mouseketeers*
DBR-69   *Annette sung by Jimmie Dodd*
DBR-68   *Mousekartoon Time with Donald Duck and Mickey
              Mouse*
DBR-65   *Jiminy Cricket—Safety First*
DBR-64   *Mousekemusicals—Darlene Gillespie*
DBR-63   *Roll Up the Rug for More Mousekedances*
DBR-62   *Mousekethoughts—Jimmie Dodd*
DBR-59   *Corky and White Shadow—Darlene Gillespie*
DBR-58   *Spin & Marty—Complete Story in Song*
DBR-56   *Jiminy Cricket Sings 5 Songs*
DBR-55   *Mouseketunes*
DBR-54   *6 Mousekedances and How to Do Them*
DBR-53   *Fun with Music from Many Lands*
DBR-52   *Fun with Music Vol. II*
DBR-51   *Fun with Music Vol. I*
DBR-50   *Mickey Mouse Club March*

PUBLICATIONS AND COMIC BOOKS

Little Golden Books in foreign languages published abroad.

Jiminy Crickett Fire Fighter	(D-50)	France	3/1956	
Goofy, Movie Star	(D-52)	France	6/1956	
		Sweden	1/1957	Cover
		Yugoslavia		Cover
Mickey Flies the Christmas Mail	(D-53)	France	12/1956	
Mickey Mouse and the Missing Mouseketeers	(D-57)	France	2/1957	
		Sweden	10/1963	
Donald Duck and the Mouseketeers	(D-55)	France	12/1956	
		Mexico	2/1965	
Donald Duck Safety Book	(D-41)	France	2/1955	
Donald Duck Prize Driver	(D-49)	Sweden	3/1956	
Donald Duck in Disneyland	(D-44)	France	6/1955	
		Sweden	5/1958	Cover
Little Man of Disneyland	(D-46)	France	11/1955	
		Sweden	5/1958	
Davy Crockett's Keelboat Race	(D-47)	France	12/1955	
Robin Hood	(D-48)	France	2/1956	

ONE SHOT COMIC MAGAZINES
1956 *Corky and White Shadow*
1956 *Spin and Marty (The Boys Who Rode for the Triple R)*
1956 *The Nature of Things*
1956 *The Hardy Boys*
1957 *Spin and Marty (Their Friendship Was Genuine, But . . .)*
1957 *Jiminy Crickett*
1957 *Spin and Marty (Big Chief Whirlybird)*

MISCELLANEOUS COLORING BOOKS
1955 *Walt Disney's Mickey Mouse Club Box of 12 Books Color*
1955 *Mickey Mouse Coloring Book*
1956 *Mickey Mouse Club Coloring Book* (2nd Design)
1957 *Mickey Mouse Club Coloring Books* (3rd Design)
1957 *Mickey Mouse Club Dot-to-Dot Coloring Book*
1956 *Mickey Mouse Club Giant Funtime Coloring Book*
1956 *Mousekartoon Coloring Book*
1956 *Spin and Marty Coloring Book*
1956 *Jimmie Dodd Coloring Book*
1957 *Jimmie Dodd Magic Carpet Coloring Book*
1957 *The Hardy Boys Coloring Book*
See also: "Personalities"

LITTLE GOLDEN BOOKS
1955 *Little Golden Book, Mickey Mouse Edition* (MMC 24 pp. D-67)
1953 *Mother Goose* (D-51 is MMC edition. D-79 is reprint of D-51)
1954 *Donald Duck's Safety Book* (MMC edition)
1955 *Disneyland on the Air* (MMC edition)
1955 *Donald Duck in Disneyland* (MMC edition)
1955 *Little Man of Disneyland* (MMC edition)
1955 *Davy Crockett's Keelboat Race* (MMC edition)
1955 *Robin Hood* (MMC edition)
1956 *Donald Duck, Prize Driver* (MMC edition)
1956 *Jiminy Crickett Fire Fighter* (MMC edition)
1956 *Mother Goose* (MMC edition)
1956 *Goofy Movie Star* (MMC edition)

1956 *Mickey Mouse Flies the Christmas Mail* (MMC edition,
        24 pp.)
1956 *Perri* (MMC edition)
1956 *Donald Duck and the Mouseketeers* (MMC edition)
1956 *Peter and the Wolf* (MMC edition)
1956 *Mickey Mouse and the Missing Mouseketeers*
1956 *Cinderella's Friends* (MMC edition)
1957 *Bongo* (MMC)

MISCELLANEOUS
1953 *Mickey Mouse and Pluto Pup* (MMC Book, 24 pp.)
1956 *Mickey Mouse Stamp Book* (MMC Book)
1956 *Mouseketeers Try Out Time* (Tell-A-Tale)
1955 *Mickey Mouse Club Scrap Book* (1st design)
1957 *Mickey Mouse Club Scrap Book* (2nd design)

PERSONALITIES: ANNETTE, LINDA, MOUSEKETEERS
1956 *Annette Cut-out Doll Portfolio*
1958 *Annette Cut-out Doll Portfolio*
1960 *Annette Cut-out Doll Portfolio*
1960 *Annette Sierra Summer* (Fiction)
1958 *Annette—A Clue to the Mystery of the Missing Necklace*
        (Comics)
1960 *Annette's Life Story* (Comics)
1961 *Annette—Desert Inn Mystery* (Fiction)
1961 *Annette in Hawaii* (Doll Portfolio)
1961 *Annette Coloring Book*
1962 *Annette Coloring Book*
1962 *Annette—Mystery at Moonstone Bay*
1962 *Annette Boxed Paper Doll*
1963 *Annette Cut-outs*
1963 *Annette Coloring Book*
1963 *Annette—and the Mystery at Smugglers' Cove*
1957 *Mouseketeers Cut-outs*
1958 *Linda* (Hughes) *Doll Portfolio*
1961 *Starlets* (Doll Kit—4 stand-up dolls with kits.)
1963 *Mouseketeers Cut-outs*

BOYS AND GIRLS FICTION BOOKS
    1956   *Spin and Marty*
    1958   *Spin and Marty—Trouble at the Triple R*

COMICS
    1962   *Mickey Mouse Album* (one comic)
    1957   *Spin and Marty and Annette—Pirates of Shell Island*
    1957   *The Hardy Boys in Secret of the Old Mill*
    1957   *The Hardy Boys in Mystery of Ghost Farm*
    1958   *Clint and Mac*
    1958   *Jiminy Crickett*
    1956   *Corky and White Shadow*

WALT DISNEY'S MICKEY MOUSE CLUB MAGAZINE
    Volume I   issued as a quarterly in 1956: #1—Winter; #2—
                Spring; #3—Summer; #4—Fall.
    Volume II   in 1956 and 1957: #1—December; #2—February;
                #3—April, 1957.
                (Name changed to *Walt Disney Magazine* and listed
                as bimonthly.)
    Volume II   (continued) #4, #5, #6   1956–1957
    Volume III numbers 1, 2, 3, 4, 5, 6   1957–1958
    Volume IV numbers 1, 2, 3, 4, 5, 6   1958–1959